ABU

Wild Cards

My Year Counting Cards with a Professional Blackjack Player,
a Priest, and a $30,000 Bankroll

Philip Reed

Skyhorse Publishing

Skyhorse Publishing books may be purchased in bulk at special discounts for sales promotion, corporate gifts, fund-raising, or educational purposes. Special editions can also be created to specifications. For details, contact the Special Sales Department, Skyhorse Publishing, 307 West 36th Street, 11th Floor, New York, NY 10018 or info@skyhorsepublishing.com.

Skyhorse® and Skyhorse Publishing® are registered trademarks of Skyhorse Publishing, Inc.®, a Delaware corporation.

Visit our website at www.skyhorsepublishing.com.

10 9 8 7 6 5 4 3 2 1

Library of Congress Cataloging-in-Publication Data is available on file.

Cover design by Tom Lau
Cover photo credit: Thinkstock

ISBN: 978-1-63450-340-2
Ebook ISBN: 978-1-63450-904-6
Printed in the United States of America

Contents

Introduction

This isn't, as they say in the movies, "based on a true story." The following events actually happened just the way they are told here, over the space of about one year from 2012 to 2013 while playing in casinos in the United States and South America. I recorded many of the interviews and used quotes in this book verbatim. I also kept notebooks filled with details and observations as I played blackjack (this is hard to do in casinos, where writing anything down is viewed with suspicion). I carefully recorded all the winnings and losses and accurately reported those figures here. However, many of the names of the characters in this book have been changed. In the spirit of full disclosure, I should also mention that a few of the events have been rearranged chronologically to keep the story flowing smoothly. While I only talk about a handful of trips in this book, it is actually based on many more trips to Las Vegas and one trip to Tunica, Mississippi, which I didn't include in this book.

With these caveats out of the way, you are now ready to read *Wild Cards.*

Part One: The Feel of Money

Chapter 1

Learning the Count

"Mathematicians call the dealing of cards 'dependent sequential events.' I call it 'making money.'"
—Lance Humble, *The World's Greatest Blackjack Book*

The dealer spots us across the casino floor and watches us approach. As we settle onto the stools at the blackjack table, his hands automatically sweep up the cards fanned out in front of him.

"Hey guys," he says, and starts shuffling, the cards making a soft, seductive *ziiippppp* on the green felt. The dealer is a young guy, powerfully built, wearing a white shirt and vest. The tray in front of him holds neat rows of colored chips worth up to $5,000 each.

It's Sunday afternoon on the Strip and waitresses here at the Mandalay Bay Resort and Casino are hustling drinks while flashing Vegas-sized cleavage. Around us, the party is on, showcasing a full sensory experience—pounding music, flashing lights from rows of slot machines, and screams of ecstasy from some distant craps table.

"How's your day going?" Bill asks the dealer as he reaches into his front pocket for a wad of hundreds. There's a grand in each of Bill's four pockets, separated for easy access during playing sessions.

"Slow," the dealer says, looking around at what, to me, looks like mayhem. "There must be a game on."

Bill counts out ten $100 bills and lays them in front of the dealer. The dealer gives me an expectant look, waiting for me to put cash on the table.

"I don't really know this game," I tell him. "So I'm going to sit this one out."

"Smart man," the dealer allows.

Bill's cash strikes me as a lot of money. But the dealer doesn't blink. He lays the bills out on the table so the surveillance cameras overhead can record the transaction.

"Thousand coming in!" the dealer calls over his shoulder. The pit boss, standing nearby, is heavyset, dressed in a dark suit, with graying hair and a face made of granite. He grunts his approval.

The dealer places the bills over a slot in the table and then uses a money plunger to ram them down into the safe below. It's jarring to see so much money disappear so quickly and irretrievably. But it doesn't bother Bill in the least. The dealer counts out a stack of green and black chips and pushes them across the table.

The pit boss slides over to our table and eyes Bill.

"Do you have a card?" the pit boss asks. Most casinos issue player's cards to track your wins and losses and, supposedly, to award points for free rooms and meals.

"No card," Bill answers, stacking his chips.

"Want one?"

"I don't think so, thanks." Bill smiles. The pit boss smiles, too, as if they are playing a little game.

The dealer offers Bill the yellow plastic cut card and combines two decks of cards into a single stack. Bill inserts the cut card into the middle of the stack. Using the yellow card as a guide, the dealer cuts the cards in much the same way as in other card games such as bridge. Then, he puts the cards into a discard tray and, using a small notch as a guide, he slides the cut card into the remaining deck, about twenty-six cards from the end. When this yellow plastic card is dealt, the hand is finished and then the dealer reshuffles, leaving about twenty cards unplayed. The closer to the end of the deck this cut card is placed, the deeper the "penetration," and the deeper the penetration, the more accurately Bill can count the cards.

"Counting cards" is really a misnomer—Bill is actually tracking whether more high or low cards have been played and translating this into a running count, which represents his probability of winning the upcoming hand. The higher the count, the more chance he has of winning. And the more he should bet. The count also tells him when to modify his play to win more hands.

The dealer "burns" the top card, removing it, sliding it carefully across the table so Bill can't see it, and placing it facedown in the discard tray. Bill puts two $25 green chips—a total of $50—in each of two betting circles. Now, he has $100 total on the table.

"Okay, good luck," the dealer says, and raps the table with his knuckles. He begins snapping out the first cards. "You guys in town for a convention?"

"No, we're just here to relax and play some golf," Bill answers, scanning the cards. He has a total of 16 on one hand and 18 on the other. The dealer has a queen up. The dealer's other card, his "hole card," is facedown. Bill signals he wants to stand on the 18 and hits and busts on the 16. The dealer flips his hole card over to show a 7 and, according to casino rules, has to stand since he has a "hard 17." Hard hands are those that don't include an ace, which can be counted as either 1 or 11. The dealer sweeps his hand over the chips, indicating that Bill lost one hand and won the other.

No blood.

"Where're you guys playing golf?" the dealer asks, laying out a new hand.

Before Bill can answer, a cocktail waitress appears. Her breasts are nearly spilling onto her drink tray due to some unseen underwear apparatus. "You gentlemen want a drink?" she purrs.

"I'll have a martini," Bill says, placing one chip on each hand as I order a vodka tonic. Then, to the dealer: "We're playing Boulder City."

"Never played there," the dealer replies. Bill has an 11 on one hand and a jack and queen on the other for a 20. He slides out another chip, signaling he is going to double down on the 11. Meanwhile, the dealer has a 6, which is a weak card—a "bust" card, according to some players. When the first card is a 6, there's a 30 percent chance that the hole card is a 10, and that the ensuing draw—required of the dealer on 16—will bust the hand.

The dealer gives Bill one more card for the double down, but it's a 4 for only 15. The dealer draws several small cards to reach 16, and finally a 5 to bring the total to 21. He winces sympathetically.

"Ouch," he says, then quickly sweeps up all Bill's chips.

"Ever played Paiute Country Club? It's a nice track," the dealer says.

"Never have," Bill answers, pushing two chips onto each hand. I realize the count must be high, because Bill is raising his bets. So while he's been ordering drinks and chatting about golf, he's also been keeping a running count in his head. Apparently, the count is telling him he has an advantage and it is worth raising his bets. Spotting this advantage is what card counting is all about. After all, if you knew for sure you were getting a blackjack, you'd bet every dollar in your bank account.

Play continues and I'm surprised to see that Bill's stack of chips is shrinking. The dealer is sympathetic—or at least pretends to be sympathetic—rooting against the cards he deals himself. But time and again the dealer unexpectedly puts together hands that total 20 or 21 to beat Bill's 18s and 19s. I don't know the game well, but I know enough to realize Bill is down about $800. I can't imagine taking that kind of loss in stride. But Bill's face shows no emotion.

Before long, Bill is down to a small stack of chips. My inclination would be to bet less to prolong my play. But the count must be high because Bill again places two chips on each circle. The dealer gives him a pair of 8s on one hand, and two cards that total 11 on the other. The dealer's up card is a 6. Bill splits the 8s into two separate hands and, using his last chips, doubles down on the 11. On one 8 he gets a 3 for another 11. On the other he gets yet another 8. He wants to split and double but he's out of chips.

"Hold on," Bill says. He slowly stands and digs two more $100 bills out of one of his pockets. He tosses the money on the table. The dealer snatches it up.

"Two hundred coming in!" He counts out eight more chips.

Bill places his bets and now has four hands on the table totaling $400. Bill settles back on the stool. I look over at him to see if he's nervous. He takes a slow sip of his martini and returns my gaze with quiet, probing eyes.

And then he winks at me.

For a moment I struggle to interpret this surprising gesture. And then it occurs to me. *He knows what's going to happen!* The whole idea of counting cards is to predict the future, and he knows that good cards are coming.

"Good luck," the dealer says, rapping the table again with his knuckles. He gives Bill a 9 for a total of 16 on one hand. The other card is a jack for 21. The other 8 gets a queen for 18. And on the double down Bill gets a king for 20.

High cards are good for the player, low cards are good for the dealer, I recall Bill saying during one of our phone interviews before the trip. I called him several times to make sure that blackjack, card counting—and Bill himself—was really worth writing a book about. Now, lo and behold, here come the high cards in all their colorful glory. I want to cheer, but the hand isn't over. And, even though I'm a rookie, I know that, at these tables, shit happens.

The dealer flips over his hole card to reveal a 9 for 15. His next card is an ace for 16. *Jesus!* I think, and realize that I've almost stopped breathing. The dealer pauses dramatically and then lays out one more card. It's an 8 and he busts.

"Yes!" Bill says, and holds up both hands for a double high five. I slap his hands, sharing the moment. Later, he says to me, "That was gambler bullshit. I was just trying to make it look like a big win for me."

To me, it certainly seems like a big win—he won $400 on a single hand. With the $400 he bet, he now has $800 on his side of the table. He's nearly back to even money.

I don't recall exactly what happens next except that Bill keeps playing and winning. Often, he has $100 on each of his two hands. I notice that he puts the black chips, worth $100, on the bottom of the stacks of chips. This way, he tells me later, the Eye in the Sky can't see how much he is winning. Some card counters even "rat hole" chips, slipping them into their pockets when the dealer isn't looking to disguise their wins by minimizing their stacks of chips. Although the surveillance cameras are unobtrusive—little plastic domes in the ceiling every fifty feet—they are so powerful that, according to one casino manager I later interviewed, "If you laid a dollar bill on the table, I could read the serial number off it."

Finally, another player slides onto the stool at the end of our table, a young guy with long hair. He looks a little scared. He lays a few wadded bills on the table.

"Do you mind waiting for the reshuffle?" Bill asks.

The guy shrugs and looks away.

Bill keeps playing and wins a few more hands.

"I'm cashing out," Bill tells the dealer. "Color me up."

Bill is leaving because he likes to play "heads-up" against the dealer, meaning that no one else is playing at the table. With this guy joining us, he decides to call it quits. Besides, as I later learn, most card counters prefer a series of small, quick wins that are less likely to draw suspicion. Once you double your money, Bill says, it's time to walk.

Playing heads-up against the dealer is something Bill says will give you an advantage even though the blackjack instructional books never stress it. Blackjack how-to books are filled with advice for beginning players and, furthermore, the authors may have held back some of their best secrets to avoid their overuse. Regarding heads-up play, Bill believes it's important because, when the deck is filled with high cards, he wants the best chance to catch the good cards. Also, card counters want to play as fast as possible to leverage their advantage. More hands per hour results in a greater win. So when someone insists on sitting at his table, Bill finishes that round and then leaves.

"You're leaving?" the other player asks, alarmed.

Bill ignores him.

"Nice little run," the dealer says, exchanging Bill's smaller green chips for purple and black ones. I do a quick calculation and realize he got back his $800 buy-in and won $1,600 in less than twenty minutes.

The pit boss is hovering over our table, supervising the payout. He looks at the pile of chips and then at Bill.

"Enjoy your stay," the pit boss says in a neutral tone as we slide off the stools.

Bill tosses the dealer a chip as a tip.

"Thanks. And check out Paiute Golf Course," the dealer calls after us. "It's a nice track."

We walk away.

"Let's go find Father Andy," Bill says, heading toward the slot machines. "He said they had a good video poker game here."

Father Andy is the priest from Bill's church and his frequent traveling partner on trips to Las Vegas and other casino cities around the country.

Something makes me turn and look back at the blackjack table we just left. The pit boss is huddled with the dealer, glancing toward us, talking intently. The pit boss turns away and enters something into a computer. A small chill runs through my system as I realize the risks for a professional card counter aren't just about the action on the table.

Chapter 2

Blackjack Basics

"Standard Deviation can be your best friend,
or it can be a real bitch."
—Gambler's adage

Let me step back in time just a few hours and set the scene. It's earlier the same day and I'm driving across the Nevada desert, heading toward the Las Vegas airport to pick up Bill Palis, a man I know little about except that he can go to the blackjack tables and win $18,000 in a weekend. He's a professional blackjack player and a card counter, one of the world's best. He's also a former member of the legendary MIT blackjack team that took the casinos for millions.

The other things I know about Bill are intriguing contradictions: he is Lebanese but was born in South America, he was raised in the US, and, ironically, he learned card counting while serving as an education coordinator for the Catholic Church. Bill is still a devout Catholic, deeply involved in his local church. In fact, Bill often travels with the priest from his church, Father Andy, who is an enthusiastic video poker player. I'll be meeting him, too, when I pick them both up at the airport.

From the little I know about Bill at this point, he doesn't seem like the stereotypical gambler often portrayed in movies leaning over the rail of a craps table, forehead sweating, throwing dice and screaming, "Come on, snake eyes!" In fact, Bill says that once you become a card counter you are not gambling because the outcome—at least in the long run—is known. This makes you an investor, not a gambler.

As I drive, I think about Dustin Hoffman's character in *Rain Man*, an autistic savant who counts cards so well that he seems to win every single hand. I am already getting the sense that Hollywood is, as usual, distorting reality. I bring up this subject with Bill the first time we speak on the phone.

"You mean those things you see in the movies never really happen?" I ask him.

"They take everything and multiply it by ten," Bill says. His voice has both the patience of a schoolteacher and the understated emphasis of a mobster. He pauses, thinking, and then adds: "I wish someone would write a book that captured the life of a real card counter."

I am pleased to hear him say this, since, before I even called him, I was intrigued by card counting and wanted to write a book about a professional blackjack player. That's why I called Bill, to see if he would be the subject of my book. And now, in Bill's simple words, I sense his honesty, and I feel myself being drawn toward this shadow world of card counters. I'd love to tag along and view the action from a safe distance. It's what I've done most of my life as a journalist—get as close as possible to the fight without getting hurt. Sure, stray bullets hit journalists occasionally, but usually no one fires at us.

I should tell you that Bill Palis isn't his real name. Like many successful card counters, Bill uses an alias. Most of the books about blackjack are written under pseudonyms to hide the player's/author's identity; the blackjack author Stanford Wong, for example, combined his mother's maiden name with his alma mater to get his pen name. Bill says he doesn't want the surveillance staff—Bill calls them the "casino rats"—to identify him by Googling his name and the city he lives in.

As I continue driving, I check my watch and see I am on schedule to pick up Bill and Father Andy at the McCarran International Airport. Nosing my sixteen-year-old Lexus ES 300 down the long grade toward Las Vegas, I reflect on how unlikely it is that I'm undertaking this project. Before researching this book, my gambling experience was limited to a few $2 long-shots at the horse track and several disasters at the poker table. I've never really liked card games, even though the rest of my family is crazy about bridge. But while talking with Bill just prior to this trip, he drops a bomb on me.

"I can teach you," he said.

"Teach me what?"

"To count cards."

"Me?"

"Sure. Most reasonably intelligent people can learn to do it."

Bill's words stir something inside me, the offer to step out of the observer's role and get a piece of the action myself. It arouses my spirit of adventure. And it seems like actually learning to count cards would make a much more interesting book. But it also starts an internal conflict: although I'm intensely competitive, and love sports and games, I'm basically risk-averse. Besides, my mother, who passed away a few years ago, was deeply religious and hated any form of gambling. And, frankly, I've always thought casinos were for suckers.

On the other hand, I feel I might have some of the qualities necessary to learn to count cards. Even though I'm not particularly mathematical, I am analytical, consistent, and disciplined. Once I understand the big picture, I am able to gain a better grasp of the details than most people. And, unlike many gamblers, I'm not reckless, given to chasing my bets or going all-in on a hunch. I also like to think of myself as cool under pressure. In the coming year, I get ample time to test that self-assessment.

But I'm mostly fascinated by the performance-under-pressure aspect of card counting. I'm a 4.0-level USTA tennis player, a single-digit handicap golfer, and I often appear on live national television as a spokesman for one of the largest automotive websites. To me, learning to count cards sounds like a great adventure. But at the age of fifty-nine, I'm not sure how much more information my brain can absorb.

"It would be interesting to learn to count cards," I reply vaguely.

Bill takes this as an acceptance. "You're going to make so much money," he says in his soft, firm voice.

Bill tells me that winning at blackjack doesn't require a photographic memory or Stephen Hawking's math skills. It's about repetition, practice, and staying cool with hundreds of dollars on the line. He says he taught himself card counting during his lunch hour while working as an insurance agent. Four months later he could count down a deck of cards in eighteen seconds. His first time counting cards at a blackjack table he won $750 and felt he had discovered fire. In a way, he had.

"You'll like leaving Las Vegas with a grand of their money," Bill tells me after we have nailed down the details of our first of many trips to Las Vegas.

Yes, I think, *winning a grand would be fun.* Unlike those Hollywood characters, I view $1,000 as a nice chunk of change. "I'm going to teach you all the things that aren't in the books," Bill tells me. "I can show you how to make money faster than anyone else teaching this game."

Of course I want to make money. But I have a hidden agenda I don't tell Bill at first—I want to prove that I am smart. You see, while

I've done well as a writer—mainly because of my social skills—I've secretly felt mentally inferior to other people. My father holds a PhD in chemistry, and considers numbers to be some of his closest personal friends, spontaneously reeling off calculations that make my brain explode. My sister and one of my brothers were academic champions. Meanwhile, I was a failure as a student in high school and college.

I like to believe my stunted academic career is because of an early educational misfire. In eighth grade, our family moved to Oxford, England, for a year. I was dumped into the British school system, which was academically at least two years ahead of our system. I was able to wing it in English and history courses. But I was completely lost in math class, where my teacher, Miss Reid, hated Americans. She loved to send me to the blackboard, saying, "Let's see how the Yank does with *this*." There, I faced a long trigonometry problem I had no hope of solving. I stood there in dumb silence as laughter echoed through the classroom and her sadistic satisfaction grew.

Back in the US, in my senior year in high school, I watched my friends get accepted to Harvard, Dartmouth, and other real colleges, while I was rejected everywhere I applied. My mother didn't want me hanging around the house so she enrolled me in a junior college outside Boston. After two years there, my soccer coach got me into the University of North Carolina, in Chapel Hill.

At UNC, I didn't fare much better. But in my final year of college I made an amazing discovery by observing the habits of my then-girlfriend, a straight-A student. I realized that she wasn't necessarily smarter than me; she just studied compulsively. In my last semester, as an experiment, I picked a course that was supposedly one of the toughest and forced myself to study like crazy. I even imitated the study habits of my girlfriend. And I got an A. It left me wondering if my inability to pay attention in the classroom had kept me from performing well as a student. Was there something different about the way my brain processed information that held me back?

For the next seven years I worked as a night police reporter, covering violent deaths and freak accidents on the streets of Chicago and Denver. I survived this brutal initiation and far surpassed my goals as a writer, going on to publish several novels and nonfiction books. But, despite my success as an author, I still felt lacking compared to the people I admire. My wife, and later my sons, learned my secret fear and they love me anyway even as I continue to hide my weakness from the rest of the world. Apparently, I have learned to get ahead by authoritatively presenting myself to hide my underlying deficiencies. Yes, I'm a talker—a bullshit artist, if you will. But now, in this late chapter of my life, the time has arrived for me to prove myself to myself. And card counting will be a merciless test of mental accuracy. It will be a journey into my own brain, a chance to banish old ghosts.

As I begin researching blackjack I learn that it is the world's most popular casino table game, a simple, yet endlessly fascinating challenge. And it stands apart from all other casino games because it offers the best odds. More significantly, it is the only game where the cards you will get are determined by the cards that have already been played. Let me say that again, because once you wrap your mind around that concept it changes everything: you can get a pretty good idea of what cards are about to be dealt if you learn to count the cards as they are played. When the deck is "hot"—loaded with 10s and aces—the odds swing over to favor you, the player. You now have an edge, and you can raise your bets.

As Bill likes to say, "You can beat this game."

Blackjack is the only skill-based casino game. However, gamblers will still swear up and down that they have discovered a surefire system to beat craps or roulette, or baccarat. I once met an intelligent woman who calmly told me she had mastered a technique of throwing dice to get the number she wanted. But don't believe these stories. The skillful craps player might improve his odds, but he'll never have an advantage against the almighty house. And, as every gambler eventually discovers, if the odds are against you by even 2 percent, the house will slowly and surely grind you down and close you out. And you, my friend, will head back across the desert as a loser.

The goal in blackjack, of course, is simply to beat the dealer, who has to draw cards until she reaches a total of 17. (In blackjack books, the convention is usually to make the dealer feminine and the player masculine.) You are dealt two cards faceup while the dealer gets one card faceup and a hole card, facedown. Now, based on this very limited information, you have to make a decision about what to do next. You can stand (take no more cards), hit (take one or more cards), double your bet and get just one more card, or split a pair of cards and play them as individual hands.

Preparing for this Las Vegas adventure, I read *Blackjack Winning Strategy*, the MIT manual on card counting that Bill helped write. I learn that the first step is to memorize what is called "basic strategy." Like the name card counting, basic strategy is also a bit of a misnomer since it's far from being *basic*. Although the principles are pretty simple, there are over 270 different plays to memorize.

Based on computer calculations, basic strategy maintains that for every hand dealt to you and the dealer, there is one mathematically correct response. Once you learn to play perfect basic strategy you cut the house advantage to one-quarter of a percent. Some of the basic strategy plays are obvious and some are counterintuitive. For example, an ace and a 7 give you an 18, a seemingly strong hand. But against a dealer's 10 you are still better off hitting. Why? Because, after playing millions of hands, the computer shows that you win more often by taking another card. Other basic strategy plays are borderline; you win more often hitting 16 against a dealer's 10, but statistically speaking it's very close.

Once you learn basic strategy, you'll lose money more slowly. But if you're eventually able to combine card counting *with* basic strategy, you can get up to a 2 percent *advantage* on the house.

When you have the all-important edge you bet as high as you can without attracting the suspicion of the pit boss or the surveillance staff watching through the "Eye in the Sky" cameras throughout the casino.

Despite what people commonly think, counting cards isn't cheating or illegal. But the casino has the right to throw you out if you win too much. Card counters call this getting "backed-off" or even "back-roomed." Up to the 1990s, when the mob ran the casinos, they took card counters into the basement and broke their jaws. Either that or they hired dealers known as "mechanics" to cheat the counters out of their winnings. Mechanics were so skilled, Bill tells me, that they could hold out a card and make it change into another card right in front of your eyes.

Looking at the basic strategy charts in the MIT manual, I think, *I can do this*. But instead of trying to cram basic strategy into my brain, I download a blackjack app for my iPhone and play with the basic strategy charts at my elbow. Slowly, I see a pattern to the plays I am memorizing. When it makes sense to me, it is easier to memorize.

As I warm to my new project, my wife looks on nervously while I deal blackjack hands to myself at the kitchen table and keep track of my theoretical winnings with poker chips.

Most basic strategy plays can be absorbed in a few hours. But to really learn all of basic strategy, and recall the correct plays under pressure, takes much longer. Soon, though, I begin to see that I am playing evenly with—and often ahead of—the virtual casino. I begin to itch to play for real. Shortly before my first rendezvous with Bill in Vegas, I get my first chance.

My father and I take a cruise to Puerto Vallarta, Mexico, and I discover they have a casino on board. With only shaky knowledge of basic strategy, I sit down at a blackjack table where the minimum bet is $6. With shaking hands, I win during my first four sessions and

Chapter 3

I Meet the Pro

"Casinos are like hookers. They take all your money, screw you, and then ask, 'Did you have a good time?'"
—Bill Palis

Arriving at the Las Vegas airport, I know I am nervous about meeting Bill, because I am suffering from another ill effect of being over fifty-nine: I need to hit the restroom, and I need to do it now.

I park the Lexus in a high-rise structure, walk into the airport, and find a bathroom. When I come out, I spot Bill and Father Andy waiting for me at the curb. Bill said he would have his golf clubs with him, so he is easy to spot. He is medium height with short dark hair and, as a former college football player, he retains a sense of latent power. He extends a large hand and gives me a strong handshake and a big smile.

I immediately notice Bill's outfit: cowboy boots, jeans, and a T-shirt from Memphis, all part of an act to look like a naive tourist and avoid recognition by casino security. His broad, handsome face seems friendly when he smiles, but since I know of his prodigious talents as a counter, I am looking for some physical manifestation of his abilities. I conclude that his eyes reveal his inner self. Large and penetrating, they seem to linger on me with a cold, probing quality that allows for no bullshit.

Father Andy is a tall, mild-mannered, middle-aged man whose eyes are wise and watchful behind thick glasses. He smiles often and easily but he has a serious, compassionate demeanor. I immediately feel at ease around him. But I'm also struck by a sense of incongruity: What is he doing here in Vegas with a professional blackjack player? And doesn't the Church frown on gambling? But I decide to keep these questions to myself for the time being.

The visit gets off to a rough start. I had parked the car in a hurry and can't find it, so we all make small talk, Bill and Andy dragging their suitcases behind them, as we get on and off elevators in the parking garage. Here I am, asking to learn from the Zen Master of card counting, and I can't even remember where I'd parked my damn car. Eventually, I get my bearings. It turns out there were two second floors, one with a mezzanine, and one without. We load the car and turn it toward the Vegas Strip in the distance.

In the car we make getting-to-know-you conversation. Father Andy tells me he's been putting in long hours at the church because there have been a lot of funerals. Many more funerals, he sadly tells me, than baptisms. It strikes me as an odd comment but then Bill explains: more people are leaving the church than there are joining.

"So I'm looking forward to having three days to relax and play video poker," Andy says.

"No blackjack?" I ask.

"Not me," he laughs. "I can't take the pressure."

As it turns out, Andy has his own goal for this trip.

"I'm looking for a royal flush," he says.

"What do they pay?"

"Four grand," Father Andy says, chuckling as he visualizes such a big win.

"Have you had one before?"

"Four," he says proudly. "But it's been a long while."

"So he's due," Bill eagerly chimes in. We drop Father Andy off at the Rio, where he says he got a great room rate. Bill and I head to the Flamingo, where the hassles continue. The check-in line snakes across the lobby and looks like it will take an hour. Around us, a noisy congregation of conventioneers, tourists, and bachelorettes take over the lobby. It's only noon, but people are already carrying drinks, their eyes scanning the carnival around them. There seems to be a desperate restlessness to Las Vegas visitors. Their faces have a stunned look, as if to say, "I'm supposed to be having fun but . . ." And so they mill around in hotel lobbies, in casinos, and out on the sidewalks, waiting for some diversion, some fulfillment of the promise that draws them here.

The playing tables I can see from the check-in line are mobbed. The rows of slot machines are swarmed by lever-pulling, button-punching senior citizens, pouring money into the casino system with little regard to any chance of winning. As my wife wisely observed, people want to believe there is something special about them, that a lucky ray of sunlight will shine down on just them and deliver a jackpot payoff. They're wrong, of course, but they keep playing anyway, thinking the very next pull of the lever will turn their luck around. While casino hosts court high-rolling Whales who fly into Las Vegas on private jets, it's these rank-and-file gamblers who pay the bills.

The check-in line at the Flamingo inches forward.

"How much did you bring?" Bill asks.

"Fifteen hundred," I say. I can feel the wadded twenties in my pockets that I withdrew from the ATM.

"I told you your bankroll should be two grand," he says, giving me a sharp, evaluating look.

To a blackjack player, a bankroll is a very specific amount that determines the size of your minimum and maximum bets. It has to be large enough to weather losing streaks without spending all your money.

"If I need more I'll hit a cash machine," I answer.

Bill nods and looks away. The line moves again.

A desk clerk signals Bill forward. He turns: "Meet down here in an hour and we'll head to the tables."

* * *

A short time later, we are walking through Mandalay Bay Casino, Bill's eyes evaluating the different blackjack games here.

"Do you want to play first?" Bill asks.

My stomach tightens. "What are the table minimums here?"

"I could probably find you a quarter table that has a nice two-deck game," Bill says.

For one ludicrous second I think Bill is actually referring to a quarter as in 25 cents. Of course, he actually means 25 *dollars*. And I know that Bill recommends playing two hands against the dealer—and if you do that, casinos require you to double your bet. So that's $50 on each hand. The one and only time I had played blackjack was for a $6 minimum. I swallow hard, a cartoon swallow, so loud I am afraid Bill can hear it.

"Why don't you go first?" I say casually, as if I am merely doing it out of politeness, like holding a door open for him.

At empty tables, dealers in white shirts and vests stand with their hands folded behind their backs, smiling at us as we pass, or busying themselves shuffling cards and counting chips. Cocktail waitresses scurry between the tables, plying gamblers with free drinks.

"Penetration, penetration, penetration," Bill says, watching the dealers. "It's all about penetration."

Bill's intense face relaxes for a moment and he smiles. "My wife is always kidding me, when I go around and scope out the black-jack tables. She says, 'How's the penetration, Bill?' But it's the most important step to choose a beatable game."

A few minutes later, Bill stops near an open table. "This game looks good."

"How can you tell what the penetration is? There's no one playing here."

"See the notch in the discard tray?" he says. "The dealer puts the cut card in the same place every time. If there is no notch, it's left up to the dealer, and if they don't like you, or you start winning too much, they'll cut higher and higher and your odds drop."

Besides deep penetration, computer simulations show that black-jack tables that offer the rule where the dealer stands on "soft 17" increase the odds for the player. Computer simulations reveal the mathematical odds of different blackjack decisions by instantly play-ing millions of hands and recording the numbers of wins and losses. Before computer simulations were available to show the mathematical odds of different plays, gamblers devised strategies based on intuition, personal observation, and assumptions. Case in point, when a player has two cards totaling 16, and the dealer shows a 10 card (10, jack, queen, and king are all worth 10), it seems intuitive to stand. As casual blackjack players say, "You stay you play, you hit you die." But computer simulations revealed that hitting 16 offered better odds of winning more hands in the long run.

In 1953, four US Air Force officers with an interest in blackjack and lots of time on their hands used desk calculators to examine the statistical odds of different blackjack hands. The process took three years and their results were published in *The Journal of the American Statistical Association*. Their article caught the eye of MIT Profes-sor Edward O. Thorp, who went one step further by testing their findings using a more powerful IBM computer. He devised the first card-counting system and wrote the bestselling *Beat the Dealer*, originally published in 1962. And the modern era of blackjack began.

Earlier I had asked Bill if there were other ways to choose what table to play at besides ones that offer deep penetration and stand on soft 17. He said games with varying numbers of decks also change the odds. A few casinos still offer single-deck games. Double-deck games are also available, but six- and even eight-deck games are much more common. Another thing Bill warns against is playing at tables with continuous shuffling machines, which are large black machines that are easily recognized. After a few hands, the discarded cards are placed into the machine, which reshuffles them and spits them out in a steady stream. This completely erases the advantage of card counting, and these games should be avoided entirely.

The minimum bet at the table Bill spots is $25—just what he is looking for. It is then that we sit down across from the young, powerfully built dealer and discuss the merits of Paiute Golf Course, as I described in the opening chapter. It is sobering for me, a newcomer to the game, to see how the dealer and pit boss study us carefully as we turn to leave.

* * *

"Did you see that?" Bill says as we leave the table. "The pit boss was watching me and I was watching the dealer and the pit boss at the same time while I kept the count. But I have to make my wins look lucky. If they see a pattern to what I'm doing I'll get backed off."

"How do they back you off?"

"Usually, you get a tap on the shoulder and the casino manager tells you to leave," Bill says. "But if they tell you to follow them, you better start walking in the opposite direction. You don't want them to backroom you. They might also read you the trespass act—if they catch you playing there again you get arrested."

Casinos now use facial recognition software to identify known card counters. To thwart the software, Bill grows a goatee for his trips to Las Vegas. He sometimes wears a baseball hat to make his face harder to spot, and he always removes a distinctive ring he normally wears. I look around and see there are cameras everywhere—shiny black domes looking down on us. The surveillance guys can zoom in on a person's face or track a player as he leaves the table and walks across the casino.

"You believe the way that guy sat down like that, right in the middle of the shoe?" Bill asks. "Other players are scared to play alone so they want to sit with you. They think it will make them lose more slowly."

We go into a men's room and I follow him to the end of a row of urinals. He pulls out a cocktail napkin and a pen.

"I document everything," he says, writing down his winnings, where he played, and the time. This prevents him from playing at the same place during the same shift and arousing the suspicion of the pit bosses.

"But I don't write anything down like this out there," he says. "This is the only place where there are no security cameras."

We go back outside and Bill heads for the cashier's window. A young woman in a tight red top and heels staggers up to us and looks at all the black chips in Bill's hands.

"I like your chips better than mine," she slurs, lurching toward Bill.

Bill turns away. We keep walking.

"Your wife must really trust you," I say to Bill.

"Why?"

"Well, you're alone here in Sin City, you've got money, and you have women coming on to you . . ."

"I've never cheated on Pat and I never will," Bill says. The way he says it, and his tone of voice, is like a door is closing on that subject. Bill plays cards on the principles of mathematics, and apparently he lives his life on certain principles, too. But this seems starkly out of place in a wide-open town like Las Vegas.

"Here, take my chips and cash 'em out for me," Bill says. "I don't want them to take my picture."

I take Bill's stack of black and green chips and head toward the cashier's window. I love the feel of their dull weight, as if they are expensive pieces of jewelry. I go to the cashier's window and push the chips to the woman behind the bars. She counts out a long row of $100 bills, recounts it, and then pushes the stack across to me. I have a flashback of the dealer ramming Bill's money into the safe below the blackjack table. Now, here it is, back again, more than doubled. That's what I call a good return on investment.

I take the bills, wishing they were mine. I hand the money to Bill and he allows himself a grin.

"Sixteen hundred bucks for a half hour of work," he says. "Tell me what kind of lawyer makes that kind of money?"

"What do you do, put it in your mattress?"

"Ten percent goes to charity."

"Charity?"

"My church, or other sources. I feel I've been given this gift so I need to give back."

"And the rest of it?"

"I buy retirement CDs."

"Nice. How much do you have socked away?"

He stops. It's the first time he's balked at any of my questions.

"That's classified," he says. Then he smiles. "But it's well into six figures."

We're outside now and the fresh air feels good. The sidewalks are packed with people and the lights are exploding around us. Nearby, the fountains outside the Bellagio soar into the night sky. I've got all kinds of adrenaline pumping through my system from watching Bill play, from holding so much cash, and from seeing his victory with my own eyes.

"So what's next?" I ask.

"I have a little ritual I'd like to share with you," he says. "I like to win just enough to buy a nice bottle of wine with their money. You up for that?"

"Let's do it," I say. Seeing Bill win has given me a giddy contact high. And that high is called *easy money.* "Let me call Father Andy and tell him to meet us there."

A half hour later we approach the high-stakes tables at the Bellagio. The $100 tables are empty tonight. Bill lays out a grand as I stand behind the table with Father Andy and watch. The dealer is a perky young woman named Lizzy.

"Is that short for Elizabeth?" Bill asks with two chips on each hand for a total bet of $400.

"That's my real name," the dealer chirps. "But it seems too formal to use here."

Lizzy starts dealing. Bill gets a 15 on one hand and a 17 on the other. He stands on both hands against the dealer's 6 and wins.

"Nice!" the dealer chirps, paying Bill with black chips. "But you never know about this game. It can definitely bite you."

"Now you're making me nervous," Bill says laughing, playing the part of an inexperienced gambler.

He stays even for a few more hands and then gets a split and a double. He wins both and stands up.

"You're cashing out?" the dealer says, looking worried. The pit boss has drifted over and is monitoring the situation.

"You made me nervous," Bill says. "I'll take a win this time 'cause I know I'll give it back tomorrow." Later, I learn that all card counters have to talk like fatalistic gamblers. They magnify any loss and downplay all wins.

At the cashier's window Bill gets his grand back with an extra $800. That means he has won $2,400 after less than an hour of play.

"Now we enjoy a nice bottle of wine on their money," he says.

"I am so jealous," I moan as I watch him pocket the money. "I want to do that."

"You will," he says. "I'm telling you, your time will come. You're going to make so much money doing this."

The three of us settle in at the wine bar and Bill selects a California Cabernet for $93. When it arrives we toast and savor the complex flavors of an exquisite wine. Or does it just taste so good because Bill bought it with *their* money?

"Okay," I say. "Maybe I can imagine learning to count cards. But how the hell can you learn to be so icy under pressure?"

"Pressure?"

"Come on. Back there you had $400 on one hand. If I did that I'd be shitting bricks."

I quickly look over at Father Andy to see if he's offended by my language. But he just laughs.

"I'd have a coronary," Andy says. "Sometimes when I'm watching Bill play, I just have to walk away."

Bill smiles, enjoying this. But he turns serious.

"Pressure is relative."

I wait for more.

"If you knew what I went through to get here . . ." he says.

I tilt the bottle to show him there is a lot of wine left and I'm interested in hearing his story. He relaxes, changing gears, and looks into the past.

"Counting cards isn't illegal," he begins. "But you have to learn to lead a secret life."

Chapter 4

The Big Player

"The Court finds little difference between a slot-cheat who uses a crowbar to pry open a slot machine and a card counter who uses his mind to pry open a deck of cards at casino blackjack."
—A Nevada judge in a ruling that was later overturned

t's the late 1990s and Bill is playing a two-deck game at a $100 table at the Mirage in Las Vegas. He has been counting cards for about four years now and his winning ratio is steadily rising. He doesn't meet other card counters face-to-face, but he swaps messages with them in different online forums, trading tips about new card-counting strategies, casinos that have good games, or those that have tight security.

Now, playing heads-up against the dealer, Bill watches as the count shoots up for the first time in three shoes. He wants to increase his bets, spreading from his minimum bet to $500, but first he glances around to check for heat, to see if any pit bosses are watching.

The coast is clear. The only thing he notices is a heavyset guy standing a few feet behind the tables watching him play.

He's probably Wonging, Bill thinks, sliding five black chips onto both circles. *Wonging* gets its name from Stanford Wong, author of *Professional Blackjack* and one of the legends of the game. Sometimes called "back counting," Wonging is when a player stands behind the table counting cards and then jumps in and bets when the count gets high.

Bill refocuses on the cards. He gets a 15 against a dealer's 10 but this time, because the count is so high, he knows he shouldn't hit. It's one of eighteen "indexes" he uses to modify basic strategy. Sure enough, the dealer flips over a 4 for 14 and then hits and gets an 8 for 22.

"Too many," the dealer says, paying Bill with a stack of black chips.

That 8 would have busted Bill's hand, so knowing the index play earned him $500. Index plays are used by expert card counters to further improve their advantage. As the count rises and falls—showing that there are either more high or low cards in the deck—the correct basic strategy play changes. For example, if the player is dealt a 16 and the dealer is showing a 10, basic strategy says to hit. However, as the count rises, signaling that many high cards are about to be played, the card counter should stand on 16 to increase his chance of winning. A few hands later the count shoots up again. This time, Bill gets a blackjack on one hand and a 19 against a dealer's ace.

"Insurance?" the dealer asks.

"Even money," Bill answers. Normally, insurance is a sucker bet. But when the count is high it pays off. Instead of paying for insurance, Bill says "even money" to show that he'll take the blackjack at even money, rather than 3 to 2. It's just a different way to pay for insurance. Sure enough, the dealer has a blackjack too, so Bill still wins money, albeit at a lower rate.

There is a prickling feeling on the back of Bill's neck so he turns and sees the heavyset guy still watching. Only now the guy is smiling at him. What the hell is he up to?

"You know what? I'm done here," Bill tells the dealer, gathering up his chips. He turns to look at the man more closely. He's a roly-poly kind of a guy with bright eyes and a humorous, knowing expression. Then the man nods his head toward the exit and starts walking. Bill follows at a distance.

Outside, the man keeps walking until he passes the valet parking stand. It's dark, but the concrete around them still radiates the heat of the day. The man turns.

"Bill?" the guy asks in a low tone.

"Yeah," Bill says. "You must be Ed."

"Yeah, but we can't talk here. There's a pizza place, Francelli's, about a mile west on Tropicana. Meet there in thirty minutes?"

"Sounds good."

They separate. Bill gets his rental car from the valet and a half hour later he's sliding into a booth across from Ed in a family-style pizza joint, far from the Strip.

"Good to finally meet you," Bill says. "I thought that must be you, but you never know."

Earlier that week Bill had been online, trading messages with Ed, and told him the Mirage was one of his favorite places to play. Ed, who, like most serious blackjack players, uses an alias, runs a gambling bookstore in Las Vegas; he dropped into the Mirage looking for Bill.

"When I saw you take even money with a plus-8 count I was pretty sure it was you," Ed says. "You don't see many ploppies make that play."

Bill laughs at Ed's use of that word. A ploppy is a player who plops himself down and plays without any idea of what he is doing.

For the next half hour, Bill and Ed chat about themselves, their families, where they live.

Then, it's back to business. Ed leans forward.

"I have a question for you," he says. "Are you interested in joining the Advantage Players Club? I've talked to a few of the guys and they think you'd make a great member."

Bill has heard of the club, a secretive invitation-only organization of the best blackjack players in the world.

"That'd be great," he says. "When's the next meeting?"

"Hold on," Ed says. "I don't mean to be a jerk, but we need to do a full background check on you first. Sorry, but there have been some casino security guys who have tried to infiltrate our group."

"Sure, I understand," Bill says. "Do what you gotta do."

"Anyway, if it all checks out then you come to our next meeting. The way it works, we let you know what the dates are, and you fly out here. Then, about twelve hours before the meeting, we let you know where the meeting is going to be held."

"I get it—more precautions," Bill says, enjoying the intrigue.

A month later, Bill flies into Las Vegas on a Thursday night, jumps in a cab, and goes straight to the restaurant, where the meeting is already underway in a private area in the back. An intense discussion about a new card-counting system is in progress. Bill listens as the group discusses the pros and cons of the different system until someone says, "Look, I've got a deck of cards—let's try it out." The members huddle around a table while they play out several hands and test the results.

The other members, all first-class card counters, are from every walk of life: college professors, statisticians, financial analysts, and even astrophysicists. Most of the members have lavish lifestyles; one guy has a collection of rare cars he had bought with money he took off of the casinos. Bill is completely in his element.

"It was a secret club, a fraternity, and the camaraderie was fantastic," Bill tells me, sipping his wine in the Bellagio. "We were all making a lot of money but for all the right reasons. The meetings were at night so during the day, we were free to play as much as we wanted. We used to play and make a couple grand until we got thrown out. It was a great time."

One year later, Bill goes to a costume ball put on by the Advantage Players Club. Two guys dressed as characters from the movie *Men in Black* approach him and ask him to step outside for a few minutes.

Removing their masks, one of them says, "We're hearing really good things about you."

Bill nods, trying to guess where this is going.

"We wondered if you wanted to go to the next level."

"What level is that?" Bill asks.

"Team play. We'd like to recruit you for our team. The MIT team."

Bill's pulse shoots up. He's heard a lot about team play, even though this is before the book *Bringing Down the House* or the movie *21*. Multiple players, called the "counters," enter a casino separately and play at different tables, betting the minimum and keeping the count. When the count shoots up, and the deck gets hot, they give a signal to call in the "Big Player," who sits down and places the maximum bet on two hands. From the point of view of the Eye in the Sky, it appears that a high roller sat down and just got lucky. Using this strategy of designated counters and Big Players maximizes the mathematical advantage of card counting. Basically, it means that the big bets are in play only when the count is very high. And it also removes the chance of detection by the Eye in the Sky.

"I'm in," Bill replies. "What's the next step?"

Several weeks later Bill meets the two men, Steve and Brian, in a hotel room near La Guardia Airport outside New York City. They ask Bill to take a test to prove he can use the Hi-Lo counting system and memorize eighteen different index plays. After Bill aces the test, the guys have one more question: Does he have a problem with taking a lie detector test?

Bill shrugs. "I've got nothing to hide."

"Great. Okay, here's how it works," Steve says. He explains that they find investors and guarantee them a percentage profit that is greater than what is currently available through other financial sources, such as on the stock or bond market. They use the investor's money—usually between $100,000 to $150,000—until they "break the bank" by covering the promised profit. Then the team is paid in a variety of different splits. Besides the twelve-member team Bill played on in Las Vegas, the MIT people had teams simultaneously playing in Biloxi, Atlantic City, and Europe.

"We want you as a Big Player, okay?" Steve says. "You have a cool head and you don't get rattled. But we want you to go on a few trips first as a counter, just so you can get familiar with how we do things, what the flow is."

"Sounds fair," Bill says.

"If things work out," Brian adds, "we want you to help us recruit and train the other players. Your background as a teacher will be a real plus there."

Bill had begun his career as a teacher but turned to other things when he was briefly laid off. For years he remained active as an educational coordinator in his church.

A week later Bill is at work in his office, answering questions from clients about investment funds and money market accounts, when a new email hits his inbox. It's from Brian announcing the next trip to Las Vegas for the MIT team. It goes to the email addresses of nearly one hundred counters and Big Players, and whoever answers first gets the openings for the trip. Bill responds immediately, saying he wants to go. He books a flight and tells his wife he'll be out of town for the weekend.

That Friday, he flies into Las Vegas and takes a cab to the hotel. Later that night, he meets the rest of the team members in a condo near the Strip. Looking around the room he sees he's much older, a dinosaur by comparison to all the college-aged counters. But he also feels confident he can out-count them all.

The team is loaded with real characters. Danny Chang, one of the team's founders, is an absentminded genius. Once, when Chang and his wife, also a card counter, were preparing to move to another apartment, his wife spotted a cardboard box marked "trash." She was about to throw it in the dumpster when she felt something rattling around inside. She opened the box and found $70,000 worth of chips from the Caesar Casino in Las Vegas that they could still redeem. Alarmed, she began opening all the boxes. In another, also marked "trash," she found an envelope containing $200,000 in cash. When she told Chang about it, his only comment was, "Yeah, I remember we were a little short on that last bank."

The team leader assigns Bill to work with a Big Player named Jason and they review the signals used when the count is high. They decide to hit the Mirage first.

"Here you go," Brian says, handing Bill $5,000 worth of chips. "Play your minimum bet and just keep the count. When the count is plus 3 give the signal and Jason will do the rest."

"Plus 3?" Bill asks, surprised. "You can spread your bets at plus 1 and make good money."

"We know that," Brian says. "We need a deep count to make sure there's time for the Big Player to make it to the table, and get his bets down. At plus 1 it could just dip back into the negative."

"Ah," Bill nods. "Good point."

They split up and head over to the Mirage, an elegant hotel casino in the middle of the Vegas Strip with a glass atrium looking up at the night sky. All the counters enter the casino separately so the Eye in the Sky doesn't connect them. Once inside, Bill spots the other team members in the high-stakes area. It's a Saturday night, about ten at night, and the casino is jammed.

"I was a little nervous the first night," Bill tells me, pouring more wine. "I wasn't worried about keeping the count—I knew that inside and out. But the casino security guys were really nervous about team play, and they were looking for us or a couple of the other teams. Sometimes we ran into the Greek or Czech teams and whichever team got there first, stayed.

"Once I was at the table and started counting I lost all my nervousness. Everything went smooth that weekend and the team made $35,000. I'd never seen so much money before. I went on three trips as a counter and then Steve and Brian let me know they wanted me to move up to be a Big Player."

This was a busy time for Bill because his children were in middle school, his wife was a full-time teacher, and his investment business was starting to take off. Still, he was hooked on the adrenaline rush of team play, the high stakes, and the camaraderie. And now he had the challenge of being a Big Player. So he headed back to Vegas, and they asked him to supervise a team of four counters.

The team chooses the MGM Grand for Bill's first night as a Big Player. After they review the signals, he lets the counters enter the casino first and get in place. Then he follows, taking $15,000 in chips from Steve. The pit at the MGM is huge and the tables are jammed with high rollers. Bill takes up a position nearby among the slot machines where he can see all the tables at once. He reaches into his pockets, touching the chips, and *waits*.

Then it happens. Simultaneously, all four counters give the signal.

"And I froze. For some reason I just stood there and stared and couldn't move. I guess I was completely unprepared for this to happen. Finally, I snapped out of it and I hustled over to the first table. 'How's the table?' I ask when I sit down.

"'Ugly,' the counter answers. 'I've won zero hands since I got here.'"

Zero is the signal they use to say the count has dropped. So Bill realizes he has missed his chance.

"I guess I'll try another table," Bill says, picking up his chips. He moves to the second table with a high count. Only when he gets there, that count has also dropped. At the third table the count has dropped too. And when he tries the fourth table it is closed because someone had spilled a drink on it.

"That was a crappy introduction to being a Big Player," Bill says. "But pretty soon I made up for it."

A short time later, a counter calls Bill to a table with a plus-4 count that calls for a $2,000 bet on two hands. He wins them both, keeping the updated count in his head. The team leaders had told him to stay at a table and play as long as the count was positive. So now, with the count at plus 7, he bets two hands of $5,000—the table maximum.

"It was funny because, when you lay out that kind of money, everyone freaks out," he says. "Some people get scared and leave the table. Others get this huge smile on their face like, 'Wow. This is going to be fun.' I remember that the dealer got really nervous and had to look at his own little sign on the table to see what the maximum bet was. But he still didn't know if it was allowed so he called the pit boss over to approve my bets."

Bill gets a pair of 8s on one hand and an 11 on the other. The dealer is showing a 10. Bill splits the 8s and gets a third 8. He splits again, putting down another $5,000 in chips. He also doubles down on the 11. When Bill is finally done placing all his bets he has $35,000 on the table.

"The word went out that something big was going down," Bill says, "and this huge crowd started forming behind me. Even the cocktail waitresses stopped serving and just stood there watching. There were two pit bosses watching and I knew the Eye in the Sky was watching too, of course. My heart was really pounding.

But despite all that, I still had to make the perfect play. And that wasn't so easy because on one hand I had a 15 against the dealer's 10. Normally, I'd hit that, but because the count was so high, there was a good chance of getting a 10. So I had to stand.

"Finally, it was the dealer's turn to play. I could see the dealer's hands were really shaking. He turned over his hole card and it was a 10 for 16. That was good because he had to hit. I was just praying that the next card wasn't going to be a 5 for a 21 and just blow me off the table. But I knew the count was high and, sure enough, as soon as the card hit the table I could see it was this beautiful picture card. He busted and everyone behind me went nuts.

"That was sweet," he adds. "I mean, it was like winning a car. Come to think of it, my first home was less than $35,000."

But getting paid isn't so easy.

"Sir, we can't pay this kind of money unless you have a card," the pit boss tells him.

"No problem," Bill says, producing a fake ID. He fills out the paperwork under an alias, with the two pit bosses acting as witnesses to make sure the payout is accurate.

"Now here's the funny part—I knew the count was still high. And they constantly drummed it into us that you never leave a table where the count is high. But I left anyway. It was the only time that I violated that rule. I just felt I had to get away from there and make sure I brought home that $35,000. No one ever complained and I never again left the table with a high count."

One of the toughest parts of being a card counter is developing an act to cover the high bets. Soon, Bill learns to play the part of a drunk. He orders a martini and then pours out the liquor in the bathroom and refills it with water, leaving the olive in the glass. He learns to slur his words and act like a rich, obnoxious drunk, swilling booze and spilling his drink all over the place. After he wins a big hand he claps and yells, "I don't believe this shit!" And his act has to be extra good because when he goes against basic strategy, it could tip off the security that he was counting cards. For example, no one splits 10s. But with the count high, it's a quick way to make a small fortune.

"I always started with $15,000 in chips," he says. "But sometimes I lost all that on a couple of hands. Then, I'd have to go to the back of the casino, or outside somewhere, and call the chip runner for more chips."

Team play is so effective because it maximizes the law of big numbers. With a group of twenty to twenty-five people all putting in four hours each night, you can get on the good side of the mathematical bell curve and beat the game. This means that a Big Player like Bill never bets on negative hands. Instead, his advantage is often over 2 or 3 percent. It doesn't sound like much, but it turns the tables on the casinos and wins millions for the team.

Trying to keep the heat off—the scrutiny from both pit bosses and casino security—proves to be a constant struggle. Using the lure of comps for rooms, meals, and shows, the pit bosses keep trying to figure out who Bill is. In some cases, he uses fake IDs from conventioneers that the team finds lying around the hotels. Occasionally, he even says he's from the CIA or the FBI.

"If you told them you were a Fed, they were afraid of you and let you do anything you wanted," he says. Once, a frightened pit boss, believing Bill to be a government agent, gave him a comp for dinner for $700. Three of the team members used the comp to order drinks, steaks, wine, dessert, and after-dinner drinks—and they still didn't exhaust the entire amount.

Around two in the morning, the team typically goes back to the condo and turns in all the chips. They count the money carefully to keep the team members from skimming from the profits. But once the bookkeeping is done, they go to a bar until four or five in the morning and drink and talk about the night's action. Often, Bill gets up the next morning to play on his own and picks up an extra three or four grand on each trip.

The team play isn't always fun and games. Sometimes they play all weekend and still lose $20,000 of this investor's money. But most of the time it was just a blur, three days that fly by and leave Bill exhausted when he comes home Sunday night. Come Monday morning, sitting behind his desk at work, his officemates ask, "So what did you do this weekend?" He answers, "Not much—cut the grass and relaxed." But in his mind, he's recalling $5,000 wins and staying out until dawn drinking and clubbing around Las Vegas.

"So you ask me how I learned to handle the pressure," Bill says, finishing the last of wine. "I guess I got used to putting down some pretty high bets. Now, four hundred bucks seems like peanuts."

He reconsiders this statement and frowns. "Bad answer. Let me put it this way: when the count is high, you make the right bet. That's all. You let the math tell you what to do. Then you just accept the consequences."

Simple, concise, believable. I can see a stack of chips piling up in my future.

I'm sold. "So what's next?" I ask.

"What's next?" Bill pauses, studying me. "Well, now it's your turn."

Chapter 5

A Rookie Move

"The best way to leave the casino with a small fortune is to arrive with a large one."
—Gambling proverb

had imagined that going into a casino with Bill would be like going into a tough bar with a UFC fighter—I could challenge the biggest guy to a fight knowing I couldn't get hurt. But now that I am here in Las Vegas, and I see the enemy face-to-face, I realize it won't be easy, no matter who is watching my back. The casino wants my money, and they've honed an excellent system to suck every last dollar from my wallet.

Casinos are run by the greediest people on the planet and they have no intention of letting anyone win consistently. In the last two decades, the staggering profits of casinos have caught the hungry eye of corporate America and they are now sprouting up like weeds across the country. Beginning in the 1990s, control of the casino business moved from the organized crime families to corporations.

MGM Resorts International, which built the MGM Grand on the Strip, owns many other casinos across the country. And then there is also the explosion of Native American casinos. Currently, there are some fifteen hundred casinos in the US raking in amazing profits. In 2009, for example, the casinos on the Las Vegas Strip alone took in a staggering $5.5 billion from gambling. Accelerating out of the recession, February 2013 was the single most lucrative month ever recorded in Las Vegas. Think about all the quarters lost by little old ladies at the slots and all the $5, $10, and $20 bills thrown down by craps shooters, roulette players, and other gamblers. This is a business in which people flock through your doors, throw money at you, and, ninety-nine times out of a hundred, get nothing in return except free drinks and a few kicks. Welcome to the casino business.

That's why I had never been drawn to casinos in the past: I don't have a lot of money and I like to hold onto what I have. I did, however, have one amazing experience some years ago that showed me the seductive power of gambling.

I was leaving for a convention in Las Vegas, walking out the door of my Santa Monica, California, office, when the owner of our company hailed me.

"Mr. Reed," he said in his British accent. "Will you be at a gaming table tonight?"

"I'll be in a casino," I answered. "But I don't gamble."

"I want you to listen very carefully," he said, taking a $100 bill out of his pocket and handing it to me. "Get $5 chips with this and cover the following numbers." He began rattling off the numbers he wanted me to bet on.

"Wait, wait, wait." I scrambled for a pen and wrote the numbers on a sticky note. I put the numbers in my wallet along with my boss's $100 bill.

"Now," he continued. "Go to a roulette table and cover those numbers. Play them until your initial investment is gone. Then—and this is very important—when you have exhausted the initial $100, cash out and leave. Do you understand?"

"Got it."

That night, at a roulette table in the Flamingo Casino—where Bill and I stayed on our first trip to Las Vegas—I covered the numbers my boss gave me and lost the first spin. I covered the exact same numbers again and watched as the ball settled into number 11, one of the numbers I'd bet on. The croupier slid a pile of chips toward me. It paid 39 to 1 so my $5 bet returned about $200. I covered the numbers again. *And I hit 11 again!* The croupier gave me even more chips. Now, I only had a few of my initial chips left. I covered the numbers one last time and lost. I slid my hefty stack of chips to the croupier.

"I'm cashing out," I said.

The croupier looked surprised. "But you're on a hot streak."

"I'll take the money and run," I said, with what I thought was a wry smile, intoxicated by my wins.

Moments later, the cashier counted out five $100 bills. I folded them carefully and put them into my wallet. Days later, when I got back to the office, I waited until my boss was in a meeting with other executives in a board room. I walked in unannounced.

"Mr. Reed," the owner said seeing me enter. "How did you fare in Las Vegas?"

I pulled out the five $100 bills, spread them on the table in front of him and his associates, and left without a word. I mean, as the cliché goes: money talks and bullshit walks. Five hundred dollars in cold cash did the talking for me, proving to my boss and his associates that his "system" worked.

At first, I thought I had been given some magic formula for roulette and was tempted to race back to Las Vegas to try to make a fortune. But then I looked up the actual odds for roulette. It turns out that the house advantage in roulette with a double 00 (some wheels have a single 0 and others have 00, which drops the odds even further) is 5.26 percent. So how did I win? Luck. But if I had continued playing my "hot streak," as the croupier labeled it, I would have slowly lost. This is what Bill calls the law of large numbers. The longer you play, the more the odds settle out to the true level.

A better way to understand this is to consider what happens when you flip a coin. The odds are exactly 50/50. But if you flipped a coin ten times the result would not necessarily be five heads and five tails. In fact, the coin could land heads up all ten times. However, if you flipped it a thousand times, the result would be approximately 50 percent.

Few people seem to understand this concept. Ask your friends this question: If you flip a coin and it comes up heads ten times, what are the odds of getting heads on the eleventh toss? The answer is that the odds are still exactly 50/50. After all, the coin doesn't have a memory. Each flip of the coin is a separate and unique event. And this is true of rolling dice and spinning a roulette wheel.

But it isn't true of blackjack. That is, if you count cards.

For me, that's what makes blackjack uniquely appealing. I like to look for an angle, for strategies others don't use. I like to buck the establishment and beat the house. As my wife says, "You like to mess with people." Card counting connects with these mischievous desires. And for the first time in my life, I've got a little money to experiment with. My sons are nearly done with college, my wife and I both work, and our expenses are low.

Father Andy decides to turn in for the night while Bill and I head off to play my first blackjack session of this trip.

As we sit at an open blackjack table at the Cosmopolitan Casino, I have trouble letting go of my roll of $20 bills. I feel my heart pounding as I realize I will be playing at a table where the minimum bet is a quarter—and I don't mean 25 cents. A single bet is $25, the cost of a nice meal.

"Remember the signals?" Bill asks, lowering his voice as we approach the table.

"Sure."

We've agreed that I'll play basic strategy—deciding the play on each hand—and Bill will nudge my leg under the table when the count gets high. He'll hit me once to move from $25 to $50 bets, twice to go to $75, and three times to go to $100, my maximum bet.

Weeks ago, Bill had suggested that I learn the simpler "Knock Out" counting system, or KO, which takes its name from the initials of the authors of *Knock-Out Blackjack*, Ken Fuchs and Olaf Vancura. He tells me it is a good starting place but isn't as powerful as the systems he uses. There are at least twenty major card-counting systems in use today. Bill knows them all and can switch between them to optimize his advantage in different single-deck, two-deck, and six-deck games. I've practiced the KO count at home, but I'm a long way from actually counting cards in a casino.

I lay out my $500 in wadded twenties and watch as the dealer, a tall guy with a bald head and a long face, smiles in mock astonishment at the loose bills.

"Oh my, look at all this money," he says.

Great. A joker. I wonder if he's a failed stand-up comic.

"You should have gotten hundreds," Bill murmurs, looking a little embarrassed.

Apparently I've violated one of those little etiquette rules that betrays me as an amateur. It's like playing golf with a guy who walks on the line of your putt without apologizing. But in this case it could be a blessing in disguise. In a casino, the less you act like a professional card counter, the better.

I try to keep my cool as I see my money stuffed down through the slot in the table. The dealer gives me my chips and I'm ready to go. I move a chip into each circle to signify that I want to play two hands against the dealer.

"Fifty on the first hand," Bill whispers. "Remember? On the first hand the odds are almost even."

Great! I've screwed up already. I slide out two more chips and now have $100 on this one hand. It feels a lot different than playing the $6 tables on the cruise ship or for poker chips at my kitchen table. The dealer hears Bill talking to me and raises an eyebrow questioningly.

"He's just learning to play," Bill explains to the dealer. "I'm helping him out a little."

"Sounds good to me." The dealer's seen it all. "Okay, sir. Good luck."

I get a 14 on one hand and 19 on the other. The dealer is showing a 4.

"Wave them both," Bill says.

I pass my hand over both pairs of cards to signal that I'm standing. Apparently, this doesn't pass muster with the dealer.

"Was that hit or stand? Or maybe somewhere in between?" the dealer asks with an ironic smile.

"Stand on both," I say, trying to act a bit indignant. But I know my gesture was loaded with indecision.

In casinos, the player indicates his decisions with hand signals so the Eye in the Sky can record them. To stand, you wave your hand above your cards. To hit, you tap the table next to your cards. You wouldn't think there was much to it, but when Bill played I noticed all his motions were stylish, minimal, and emphatic. He could look at a table of cards and instantly wave his hand above them as if putting a spell on them. When he wanted to hit, he would fan out his fingers and tap the felt next to the cards with just his little finger. It struck me as the height of cool. And dealers never asked him for clarification.

"Okay, moving on," the dealer says, turning over his hole card to reveal an 8 for 14. He has to keep hitting until he reaches 17 or busts. He deals himself a queen. "And I bust," he says.

I've won a quick $100 on my first hand. I'm encouraged.

"Quarter, quarter," Bill says, reminding me to drop my bet to $25 on each hand. This is the table minimum bet, and he calls it a "waiting bet" because I am waiting for the count to rise before I increase my bets again.

I win three more hands with only twenty-five on each hand. I'm up $175 in only a few minutes. I look at my growing pile of chips and recall Bill's words, "You're going to like leaving Vegas with an extra grand." The dream is coming true. This is going to be easy.

Bill hits me once on the leg and I snap back to the present. The count is higher so it's time to increase my bets to $50 on each hand. I slide out my chips and watch as the dealer gives me a 5 and a 4 for a total of 9 and a jack and a 4 for 14 on the other. He is showing an 8.

"Double and hit," Bill says. It's worth doubling on a 9 because there are so many cards worth 10 in the deck. So if the 9 gets a 10, it will be 19, which is a pretty strong hand.

Unfortunately, the dealer gives me a 3 for a total of 12 on the double down. He cocks his head and says, "Ouch." But I hit the other hand and get a 3 for a respectable 17.

Now it's the dealer's turn to play. He flips over his hole card to reveal a 6 for 14. Promising . . . If his next card is a 10 he busts. But he deals himself a deuce for 16. He has to hit again and now I'm sure he'll bust. Instead he flips out a 5 for 21.

What the hell?

"That's not supposed to happen," the dealer says sympathetically. But he quickly snatches up $150 of my chips, almost all my profit.

It's the beginning of a long slide. Time and again, my 17s and 19s are topped by the dealer putting together unexpected combinations of 20s and 21s. Just when I get a strong hand, he matches it for a tie, called a "push" in casino lingo. I just can't get any traction. I run out of chips.

"Take out another $200," Bill says.

I pull the extra money from my pocket. I'm ready for a fairy-tale ending. I imagine telling my friends back home how I rallied back and shot up and walked away after doubling my money.

But in a few quick hands I've lost another $200.

My chips are gone and I look up into the long face of the dealer. The phrase "crocodile tears" comes to mind.

"Some days are like that," the dealer shrugs. "Better luck next time."

I'm down $700 and all he can say is *better luck next time*? I stagger away from the table feeling nauseous and dizzy. I can't help but think how $700 is a round-trip ticket to the East Coast, a really nice flat screen TV, or a new computer. It could be a lot of actual *things*, except now all that money is completely gone, as if someone stuck a gun in my stomach and robbed me.

We're standing between long rows of slot machines. Around me the chaos continues unabated with conventioneers and little old ladies frantically making bets, pressing buttons, and staring at spinning symbols.

"You okay?" Bill asks softly.

I take a deep breath and try to sound brave. "Well, I'm not gambling with my grocery money."

He studies my face, as if to see if my comment is honest. Finally he says: "That's what I wanted to hear."

I'm a little surprised Bill isn't more sympathetic. On his advice I just blew $700. If I did that to someone, I'd be falling all over myself apologizing. But it doesn't seem to faze Bill. It's only much later that I understand this moment.

We start walking.

"Your hands were shaking when you reached for your chips," he says.

"Really?" Now I feel even more shame.

"Don't worry about it. When I was training the players for the MIT team, they were so nervous they spilled chips all over the table.

Some of them froze at the tables—they couldn't even make a decision. And I have to tell you, there isn't a counter alive who doesn't have butterflies when he first sits down at the table."

"What the hell happened? Did I do something wrong?"

"You're slow on basic strategy. And there were a few mistakes. But overall, you played okay. Did you keep the count?"

"No."

"Let's work on that. Let's go back to my room."

We are passing a blackjack table where a skinny young kid is playing against the dealer. Behind him, his friends laugh and mock him as he loses hand after hand.

"That makes me sick," Bill says, watching the spectacle. "The kid's throwing away his hard-earned money and he doesn't have a chance. And he probably told his friends he was a really good player, too. That's why I don't feel bad about taking the casino's money. They rip off everyone else."

We walk back outside. The feeling of the day's heat is still around us. The sidewalks are crowded with people laughing and drinking. A limousine passes in the street with a guy half out of the sunroof, shouting at the top of his lungs. Bill waves his hand toward the lights, the fountains, and the soaring buildings.

"Look at this," he says. "It's all a façade. It's all bullshit. It's here to make you think today's your lucky day. I hate it."

I realize how right he is.

"I get it now," I say.

"What's that?"

"When they say, 'What happens in Vegas stays in Vegas,' they're talking about your money."

"Come on, man. That was just your first session. You're on the wrong side of the bell curve." What he means is that even if the odds are in your favor, there are times when you will still lose.

"How do I get back on the right side?"

"Keep playing. Remember the law of big numbers? You have to put in your time."

We walk back toward our hotel. On the way I find myself thinking of how my wife will react to my loss. Before I left I told her that Bill said I'd probably make a grand.

"I'm not going to be all that happy if you make a grand," she said. "But if you lose a grand I'll be mad."

"Think of it as research money for the book," I offered.

She didn't answer. At least, not with words. We've been married for thirty years and rarely fight about money. That's because we're both pretty careful—never had much and never spent much. Still, in other ways, our finances have been a roller coaster. We moved to Hollywood in the early '80s without jobs or kids but with big dreams of striking gold as screenwriters. But when we hit the ground in Hollywood my wife lost all interest in show business. She used her master's degree in library science to keep us afloat with a part-time job in the Long Beach Public Library. With the gift of time that she so generously gave me, I wrote a play, got it staged, and attracted the attention of the producers of the nascent series *Miami Vice*. A few weeks later I held my first check for $7,000 for the story of one TV episode. After two more months I had made nearly $50,000 including a single residual payment of $20,000 for a rerun. But I never really cracked the politics of becoming a staff TV writer, where the real money is. For the next twenty years, as we raised our two sons, it was feast or famine.

Reflecting on all this after the exchange with my wife, I realize that we are all gamblers. But Las Vegas distills gambling into a single stark moment of loss or victory. Instead of gambling with the events of our lives, we are gambling with the fruits of all those events, the money we've earned or saved. We put it all on red and spin the roulette wheel or on the pass line at craps and roll the dice. If we could look five seconds into the future we would all be millionaires. But instead, we slink away from Las Vegas with empty wallets because of the lucky break we never got.

Walking along the Vegas Strip, my wallet $700 lighter, I realize, with a feeling of disgust, that I've joined the legions of defeated gamblers who came here looking for a quick buck. The casinos loom all around with their cheap lights, mocking me like a fallen fighter. But then, something occurs to me that lifts my spirits: I have Bill in my corner. And he's already gone ten rounds with Las Vegas and walked away a winner. I've still got a shot.

"Come on upstairs and we'll deal some hands," Bill says. "I'll show you some things that'll help you get your money back."

"The things they never put in the books?" I ask.

He hears his own words bounced back at him. His eyes lock on mine, probing; am I mocking him? He decides my comment is harmless.

"Exactly," he says. "The stuff no one else knows."

Chapter 6

The Hook Is In

"This is like a cross between a sporting event and a math quiz."
—Blackjack student after his first lesson

Back in Bill's room he pulls out two decks of cards and, using his $100 bills as chips, we start dealing hands of blackjack. Out the window, the sound of the Strip is now a low murmur broken only occasionally by the low boom of the idiotic pirate extravaganza at the Treasure Island Casino. From here it sounds like distant artillery fire. It's a relief to be away from all that, safe here for the time being.

"This is how I tell people to practice," Bill says. "Get some chips and cards, play the game exactly as they play it at the blackjack table, and keep track of your results."

"I just can't keep up with the speed of play," I say, as he lays out the cards.

"You will. Remember, when you first started to read you had to look at every single letter. Now you look at groups of words and instantly know the meaning. Counting cards is the same thing. You want to scan the table and know at a glance what the count is."

He deals two hands for me and one for the dealer. Only five cards in total.

"Now look at this," he says. "What's the count?"

In the Knockout System, the cards from 2 to 7 are each worth 1. The 8 and 9 have no value. The 10, jack, queen, king, and ace are all negative 1. I look at the cards. The room seems very still as I struggle with the simple process of taking the beginning count, negative 4, and adjusting it for the cards played.

Most counting systems use a "running count" and adjust it for the "true count." This is done by dividing the running count by the number of decks left to be played. The Knockout System is different because it just starts with a negative offset at the beginning of the shoe so no further calculations are required. However, many black-jack professionals claim it is not as accurate.

When I first learned the concept of card counting I was confused by the fact that the so-called "bad cards"—the low cards—were labeled positive and the good cards—high cards—were called negative. I kept thinking that negative meant *bad*. But the reason is simple: when the good cards are played they are no longer in the deck to *help* you. The smaller cards—bad cards for players—are positive because once they have been played they are no longer in the deck to *hurt* you. "Okay," Bill interrupts. "The fastest way to do this is just to use a canceling system. With two decks the count starts at negative 4. Now, we have a king and a 4—one is high and one is low, so they just cancel each other and don't change the count. We have a 10 and a 3 and they cancel. And my 8 has no value in the system so I ignore it."

"So I'm still at negative 4."

"Exactly. Now keep the count as we play out the rest of this hand." I hit on both of my hands and get low cards, so the count is now negative 2. He flips over his hole card to reveal a 3. He hits it with two more low cards, leaving the count at positive 1.

He looks at me, expectantly.

"Aren't you forgetting something?"

"What?"

"The count is plus 1. So raise your bets."

I put another bill out on each hand, raising my bets.

"So the count tells you when more low cards have been played than high cards. The deck is unbalanced, so there is a greater probability of getting the higher cards now."

"Exactly. There's no guarantee you'll win, but the probability has increased, so your bet should go up to take advantage of the situation. Remember, the way we beat this game is that we have tools the dealer doesn't. We can increase our bets and we can also double, split, and take insurance. And remember, blackjack pays three to two."

Something clicks and the fog clears just a little. We play out the rest of the shoe and I am up $200. We play two more and I finish up with $335.

"Why didn't that happen at the table?" I ask.

"It's just standard deviation rearing its ugly head."

Standard deviation is a common term with blackjack players and educated gamblers. It simply means the amount by which the odds can vary before they reach their true level. So let's say you sit down to play a two-deck game, meaning that you will be playing only about twelve hands. Of the twelve hands, you could win all of them—or lose them all. This doesn't reflect the fact that, as a card counter, you sometimes have a 2 percent advantage. But if you continued playing for ten hours, playing sixty hands per hour, the results would minimize the standard deviation that occurs in short playing sessions.

Even with the 2 percent advantage card counters sometimes enjoy, you have to weather some rough patches along the way. That's the part they don't show you in the movies. It's only by playing a longer time that the 2 percent advantage works for you. Recall the coin flip: the odds eventually get to where they're supposed to be, but you could start a session losing ten heads in a row. That's why Bill told me to bring two grand, so that I could absorb the losses and not get wiped out.

That night, as I sleep fitfully, I feel like I'm in a film noir movie and someone has slipped me a knockout drug. Playing cards float around me, and that bald dealer mocks me with an echoing voice: "Some days are like that. Better luck next time!"

I wake up early the next morning, cross the room, and pull back the curtains. Searing desert light pours in as if I've opened the door of a blast furnace. When my eyes adjust I look down to see a busy construction site below. They're putting up yet another casino.

We all meet at the Peppermill Restaurant and Lounge, where the portions are huge. Father Andy is beaming—he's up almost two hundred. Bill has won over two grand in only two sessions. I'm still nursing my wounds from my $700 loss at the Cosmo. But after a strong cup of coffee, I feel fortified and ready for another run at the tables.

Bill and I go to "downtown" Las Vegas, the old section, where he says there is a good $10 game at the El Cortez. He tells me that card counters calls it "the Sweaty Spaniard" because of the heat from the pit bosses, who hover over your table and make you sweat for every dollar you win.

As we walk down the street in brilliant sunlight, we pass transients slumped against storefronts, begging for change. They all look like they just got out of prison and are itching to kill again. It's a fitting introduction to the El Cortez at the end of the block. We step out of the sunshine and into the darkness of a time warp. It's totally old-school. The paisley carpet is saturated with spilled drinks. Broken down, compulsive gamblers stagger between slot machines, trailing cigarette ash and sour whiffs of body odor. I expect the ghost of

Sammy Davis Jr. to sit next to me at the blackjack table. Instead, Bill sits beside me as I face a stone-faced dealer of unknown nationality but with an accent so thick she might as well just go ahead and speak a foreign language. Apparently, at the El Cortez, dealers cut their teeth as they try to step up to the bigger casinos on the Strip. And some just never make it.

I'm still not able to keep a running count, so I leave that to Bill. Instead, I concentrate on more quickly making basic strategy decisions. Still, after a few promising hands, I slowly lose the $100 I bought in with. A cadaver in a baseball cap sits down at our table. It looks like he spent all his money on booze and gambling and forgot to buy food.

"Let's get out of here," Bill says.

I guess the $10 tables at the Sweaty Spaniard don't hold much interest for Bill anymore. Since he knows he can win, he wants to play the highest-stakes tables he can find. But I'm actually relieved we played the Sweaty Spaniard. As we walk back out into the morning sunlight all I can think is how much higher my losses would have been if I played the $25 tables on the Strip.

"Sometimes, when I came to Vegas with the MIT team, we'd all play all weekend and lose," Bill says. "That comes with the territory. That's why more people don't play. They don't believe the system can work."

"I guess that's where I'm at. I don't know that it works."

"You don't?" He's aghast, like I said I don't believe in God or something. It's a good thing Father Andy isn't here.

"Well, I believe it intellectually."

This elicits a knowing look. "Blackjack is a volatile game. You're never going to get away from that. But I beat it all the time. I can walk into any casino that has a good game and double my money."

I nod unenthusiastically. He takes that as a challenge.

"Okay, follow me."

* * *

Bill charges into the nearby Golden Nugget Casino, and I sit next to him as he squares off against a young and talkative Hispanic dealer. His stack of chips shrinks briefly and he asks the sullen pit boss for a couple of comps for lunch. The pit boss, who looks like he's got a second job as an undertaker, has seen Bill's losses and readily agrees. But once we have the comps in hand, Bill's stack of chips starts to grow. A few minutes later Bill tells the dealer he's cashing out.

"Did you see that?" he asks, carrying a nice stack of chips.

"What?"

"She knew I was counting and started dealing faster and faster and snatching up the cards. It didn't bother me. I can count faster than they can deal."

"How much are you up?" I ask as we head for the cashier's window.

"About $675. But I just played for fifteen minutes."

Once again, I'm so jealous.

We decide to give the blackjack a rest and play golf at a course north of town. Out in the sunlight, with a golf club in my hand, I'm revived. I feel marginally in control. I realize that's the challenge for me with blackjack—I hate being out of control.

Bill has a powerful golf swing, but today he's struggling with his tee shot. I just got new irons and I'm hitting the ball solid. *The irons, I find myself thinking, were well worth the $700 I paid for them.* Then it hits me—I've lost more than that so far at blackjack, and I have nothing to show for it. I could have bought another set of irons, or a new driver with matching woods, or maybe . . .

After our round of golf, we head back to the Strip for another run at the tables. With Bill riding shotgun in the timeworn Lexus, I drive slowly, dread growing like a sickness in my stomach. *Why, I wonder, am I putting myself through this?*

Sure enough, when we reach the Strip and find a two-deck game with a $25 minimum, I start losing almost immediately. Soon, I'm down to my last few chips. I have this horrible feeling that I'm suffocating, drowning in quicksand. I stumble away from the table after dropping another $500. Bill is quiet for a moment, respectfully letting me process the loss.

"We've all been there," Bill says. "In the beginning, when I was just learning to play, I'd get wiped out and wander around talking to myself like a crazy man. I'd be saying, 'What the hell happened? The count was high, I made the right moves, and I still got killed.'"

"What did you do?"

"I kept playing. And I saw the pattern. And once I saw it was just a pattern I knew I would be okay."

That night I sleep even worse than during the previous night. The next morning I'm numb, resigned to going through with this experiment. It's as if Las Vegas rewired my brain and disabled my ability to think straight.

I go to a two-deck table at the Aria Casino and brace myself for another beating. Instead, I win a quick $175. It's not the big win I was dreaming of, but it's a start. After Bill plays, and wins another grand, I'm ready for a second session. We find an open table at Mandalay Bay and sit down across from a friendly middle-aged dealer who could be the mom next door.

"So where're you guys from?" she asks.

"Southern California," I say. "We're just here to golf and play some cards. We're heading out in a half hour to play in Boulder City."

The pit boss turns around. She has the terse, confident manner of a bank manager. "Boulder City? Did you know Obama is coming to town?"

"President Obama?" I ask absurdly, as if it's a common name.

"Yeah. He's going to Boulder City. They're closing all the freeways."

By now I have my chips and I'm ready to go. I put two chips on each hand and win both.

"Quarter, quarter," Bill whispers, reminding me to drop my bet for the second hand.

"Yeah, he's going to tour some solar power plant out there," the pit boss says. "There's only one way into that town so everything's going to shut down."

A few hands later, I hear Bill say: "Time to rock 'n' roll." This is his signal for the maximum bet, which in my case is $75. I put three chips on each hand, get a 16 and a 14 against a dealer's 6, and watch as the dealer flips over a high card to bust.

I stand up. "You know, we better get moving," I tell Bill. But in actuality, I just want to leave the table a winner.

"Fine, let's go," Bill says.

We go to the cashier's window and I find I won $485. That means I'm up almost $700 for the day. It's amazing how this improves my mood, even though I realize I'm still down about $500 for the trip.

Miraculously, we make it to Boulder City without a hitch even though highway patrol cars are lining the route, ready to bring traffic to a grinding halt. It's like we caught the last helicopter out of Saigon. In the pro shop I discover I've forgotten my golf hat. No problem, I have a big wad of bills in my pocket and buy a brand-new hat. Life is good. And my golf game is even better.

After we finish golfing, and have a quick dinner with Father Andy (now he's up nearly $275), I can't wait to get back to blackjack. But once I'm actually at the table, I find myself facing a young female dealer who tells us she is from Afghanistan, of all places. Looking at her long face and dark eyes, I can't decide whether she is an exotic beauty or a tortured soul. My mind takes a detour, thinking of the horrors her people have witnessed over centuries of wars and invasions. Meanwhile, I get confused and forget to raise my bet when the count is high. I try to put more money down but the dealer is already in motion dealing the cards and won't allow the increased bet. She becomes impatient. Bill steps in on my behalf.

"Look, he's new to the game," Bill explains firmly. "You have to go slower."

The dealer calls over the pit boss and says, "He's getting confused and can't decide on his bets."

I'm mortified to be described in the third person like a child— "Oh, please excuse Phil, he's confused right now"—even though I know it's true.

"We'll let it go this time," the pit boss says. "Go ahead and raise your bets."

A few minutes later, still in a state of profound confusion, all my chips are gone. And so is another $500.

"But you're still up for today," Bill points out.

I realize he's right. I still have about $200. It raises my spirits just a little.

We return to Bill's room and play more practice rounds. By now, due to lack of sleep and a constant anxiety, I have difficulty paying attention. Eventually, we close up shop for the night.

When I wake up the next morning, it feels like something has rearranged itself on some deep ocean floor of my subconscious. I've accepted the losses, in the same way that death must ultimately be accepted. Finally, I rationalize that I'm paying to be trained by one of the best black-jack players in the world. When I think about it that way, my losses aren't really that bad.

I'm ready to give it one last try before I leave town after beating my head against the wall for the past three days. I count out my remaining cash on the top of my bureau. I came with $1,500 and now have about $500. I'm down a grand.

I meet Bill in the coffee shop. We check out of the hotel and I get my car from the valet. The Lexus is actually a project car from my day job as an automotive journalist. It's a 1996 ES 300 that we picked up for $3,480—barely twice my Vegas bankroll—to prove that you can buy a reliable car for short money. The teal green body is accented by light green under-cladding, and the gold kit ("*Sooooo* '90s," my younger friends tell me) still looks sharp. I want to think I look like Burt Lancaster in *Atlantic City*, a classy older guy in a classic car. In reality, I'm just another old fart in an out-of-state beater. When they make this adventure into a movie, I want to be thirty years younger and drive a Bugatti.

We stop at the Cosmopolitan, where I win a quick $175. Then, at the Mandalay Bay, I find I'm getting faster with basic strategy and can concentrate on managing my bets. Halfway into the second shoe, I hear Bill's soft, urgent voice: "Time to rock 'n' roll."

I put out $75 on each hand and have to remind myself to keep breathing. I wait, staring at the space where the cards will appear, willing them to be high cards, as the count predicts. Sure enough, I get a jack on one hand and an ace on the other. "Come on, blackjack," Bill says, patting the table next to the ace. "Come on."

The dealer gives himself a 6 and lays down a jack next to my ace. "Nice," the dealer says.

With $75 on the table, blackjack pays three to two, or $112.50.

"Let's go," I say.

"You don't want to finish the shoe?" Bill asks, surprised.

In fact, I just want to get the hell away from the table while I still have some money. But if Bill wants me to keep playing, the count must be high. I feel my mood shifting from fear to excitement. I sit back down and play out a few more hands, winning a little more. When I cash out I find that I've won another $250.

We meet up with Father Andy and get breakfast in a café with paper tablecloths. Bill writes on the paper, adding up the totals for the three days. He came with $3,000 and is leaving with $6,600.

"I usually expect to double my money so I've done all right," Bill says casually.

God, I'm so jealous.

Father Andy smiles but says nothing.

"How'd you do?" Bill probes. "You get that royal flush?"

"Believe me, you would have heard about that if I did," he laughs. "But I did all right. I made close to three hundred."

"Hey, not bad!" Bill cheers. He turns to me. "And you—you came with $1,500," he continues, "so you should have $900 in your pocket. Looks like you're down about $600."

I spill out an assortment of bills and see that he's right. So much for the exhilaration of victory. I look up and find that Bill is studying my expression, gauging my mood. I must look tired and discouraged. It's not just the money. I really hate losing. And to tell you the truth, I'm most afraid of telling my wife how much I've lost. I've always had a hard time admitting that I lost, at anything, really. I have this insane desire to always be her hero.

"When you're driving home, you'll probably start to put all this in perspective," Bill says as we head for the car. "You'll realize that this is just part of being a counter. You have to be able to take a loss and come back again without changing your plan. It's mathematics, and the numbers never change."

I know he's right—in theory. But once again I'm having doubts. It seems my subconscious epiphany the night before was short-lived. Maybe I'm not cut out for this.

The end of the visit is as ragged as the beginning. We leave late for the airport and have to scramble to get there on time. I shake hands with Father Andy and Bill, and they disappear among skycaps and departing travelers. Back on the interstate, Las Vegas shrinks in my rearview mirror until it's lost behind the mountains. I find that Bill is right. The intensity of the experience is dropping away, and the experience is falling into place, becoming distant and, as a result, more understandable.

In a burst of images from the past few days, I see Bill at a blackjack table with a stack of chips in front of him; I see a cashier counting out a long row of $100 bills; I see cards, cards, cards—and they're all jacks and aces. Finally, I hear Bill's voice as we walked along the Strip one night: "The casinos are like the guys on Wall Street—they steal every last penny you have and still want more. But I know how to get in and out and take their money. I can't tell you how good that feels."

I realize that, eventually, I want that feeling too. I'll never be as good as Bill—he truly has a gift for card counting. But what could I do if I devoted a year to practicing and playing? If I returned to Las Vegas a year later, would my hands still shake at the blackjack table? Would I eventually be enough of a threat to get backed off or thrown out of a casino? I desperately want revenge on Las Vegas. The only problem is, I don't know what my aging brain is capable of. But I am curious enough to take the journey.

I look down at the speedometer and see that these thoughts have me fired up: I've got the old Lexus up to 90 mph. I ease off the gas a little, sink back into the creaking leather seat, and roll on across the desert.

Chapter 7

Blackjack in the Andes

"Black-a-jack!"
—Dealer in a casino in San Carlos de Bariloche, Argentina

t's a month after my trip to Las Vegas with Bill and now I'm on a jet, high above the Gulf of Mexico, flying to Buenos Aires. I'm on a four-month sabbatical from my job, and I'm going to Argentina to spend time with my son, who is a graduate student there. I'm going to learn Spanish and, yes, to practice my card counting. In fact, there are casinos in the Puerto Madero section of the city that I'm eager to visit now that my $600 Vegas loss is a fading memory.

In the last month I've reached another milestone—my sixtieth birthday—and, as I consider my final decades, I know it will be important to keep my brain healthy. Research has shown that learning new skills is the best way to do this. I'm going to improve my mind by learning a new language. Actually, I'll be learning two new languages: Spanish and card counting.

In my suitcase are two decks of cards and a stack of poker chips. Bill recommended I play at least two shoes a day and keep track of the results so I'd have more confidence in the law of big numbers. Bill also suggested I buy a software program developed by his friend, Norman Wattenberger, on the website QFit.com called "Casino Verite." The software simulates the casino experience by letting you play against a virtual dealer. You buy in with imaginary money and the computer program deals blackjack hands and keeps the count. If you make a mistake, the computer will flash the correct play on the screen. It even keeps track of your chronic mistakes so you know what to practice.

Foreign languages and card counting seem to me to be closely linked mental exercises, because specific points of information need to be recalled quickly. Of the two, learning to speak a foreign language seems much harder. Just think of what happens when we have even a casual conversation with a friend. We aren't actually aware of choosing specific words (unless we are giving a speech or interviewing for a job) and yet the words readily appear on the tip of our tongue. We choose from among nearly twenty-six thousand available English words as we think at a higher level, the level of meaning.

Now look at what happens in card counting. We translate the value of the card to either a positive one or a negative one and add it to the running count. The count has to be remembered from one hand to the next and used to modify basic strategy. Meanwhile, you have to either raise or lower your bet according to the count. And all this happens as you appear casual and chat with the dealer.

A few days after I land in Argentina, I'm walking through the narrow streets of Buenos Aires, heading to my language school. I have to admit, I'm very nervous. I've always wanted to learn a foreign language. I took classes in high school and college and later listened to tapes and CDs as I commuted. But I've always had a deep feeling that I'm just not good with languages. On the other hand, my son flew to Buenos Aires and eight months later when we went to visit him, he was able to converse in what sounded to me like fluent Spanish.

Now, it's my turn.

I find the street number for my school and press the button on the intercom. A buzzer sounds and I push the door open. It's a beautiful old building with a wire-cage elevator. At the door I'm met by a young woman with various piercings who begins rapidly speaking to me in Spanish. Yes, I know this is an immersion class, but I can't understand anything she is saying. She also seems impatient. I'm led into a classroom and introduced to my professor, a tall man with curly graying hair and a calm demeanor. He slowly introduces himself in Spanish and then asks my name. I reply in my best high school Spanish. He then begins asking me other questions and I can answer some of them. I tell him I live in Los Angeles, or actually, a city to the south called Long Beach. I tell him my son lives in Buenos Aires and is a student. I tell him that, in Buenos Aires, I've rented an apartment on Avenida Corrientes. I answer all his questions and he nods, understanding me. Then it hits me: holy crap, I'm speaking Spanish!

In a fit of over-enthusiasm, I've signed up for four hours of class a day: two hours, a half-hour break, then two more hours of class. My excellent professors are German (pronounced *Herman*) and Cecilia, who complement each other nicely: German loves to discuss *futbol* and politics, and once I warm up my conversational Spanish, Cecilia moves in and kicks my ass with grammar and verb conjugations. As the weeks pass, my spirits go up and down. One day I feel I'm making progress; the next I'm discouraged by how much there still is to learn.

On my half-hour lunch break I only have time to sit on a bench on Avenida Reconquista and eat an empanada as business men and women chatter in Spanish around me. They speak quickly, naturally, with nuance, with humor. In the classroom, I struggle to get out the basics. The children in the street know more than me, for God's sake! It reminds me of how I felt sitting next to Bill at the blackjack tables, seeing him joking with the dealers, ordering drinks, and all the while keeping the count and piling up a healthy stack of chips.

During my time in Argentina, I teach my son the basics of card counting the way Bill taught them to me in his hotel room in Las Vegas, but without the $100 bills. Bill has recommended that I practice with the TV on to emulate the distractions of the casino. I find I like to have a *futbol* match on. The hysteria of the announcer and the songs of the fans are a welcome backdrop to our practice sessions. It's actually nice to have something that I can teach my brilliant son. And I'm curious to see how quickly he learns since he is a composer and a musician and is so good with languages. He asks all the right questions and picks it up quickly. Night after night, after two shoes, we find we have often doubled our money. Belief in the law of big numbers is taking root in my brain.

One night, sleepless in my apartment eight floors above the chaos of Avenida Corrientes, I begin wondering what I'm doing to my brain with all this study. Four hours of language class a day and then an hour or so of card counting. I wish I'd had a brain scan before I left so I could see if I've created new cerebral connections. One thing is for sure—I feel like I've been lifting weights with my brain. When I'm counting cards, or practicing Spanish, my brain feels like it's lighting up. I notice that it seems to pay off in other areas too. I willingly tackle abstract problems in my mind, such as adding columns of numbers and memorizing phone numbers rather than writing them down. But at the end of a long day, my brain is like a flywheel that won't stop spinning. When I lie down to sleep I see cards flying past my eyes and hear Spanish verbs changing tenses from past to present.

Online, I read that the casinos in Buenos Aires have six-deck games with continuous shufflers. I email this news to Bill and he replies with a nice note, saying he wishes he could join me in Argentina and have a nice glass of local wine. He recommends that I check the casinos anyway, since "conditions can change at a moment's notice." He concludes by apologizing for not coming down for a visit. "Who knows what trouble we could get into down there," he writes.

One night, my son and I, along with his Brazilian friend, Thiago, jump into a cab and cruise down to the casino in Puerto Madero, a flashy new section of Buenos Aires. The casino is on two huge boats with three floors of games. Walking inside, I feel the familiar rush of adrenaline and the pleasant expectation of winning money. It's a weeknight, but the place is completely mobbed. There is hardly an open seat at any of the tables I pass. And, sure enough, all the blackjack tables have the dreaded continuous shufflers.

The minimum bet is only 10 pesos. Despite the fact that Bill would call it a "bad game," I can't resist the tug of playing a couple of shoes. I buy in with 300 pesos and sit at a crowded table. A fat guy next to me is barking comments to the entire table and betting like an idiot. His humid breath is heavy with alcohol and his bulk presses into me as I try to concentrate on playing my two hands.

I slowly lose about 200 pesos over an hour of play. Still, I outlast the fat guy and many others who timidly buy in and then lose in a couple of quick hands. Something has indeed changed: I've come to see that it's all about the betting—winning the big hands and minimizing losses elsewhere. But with the continuous shufflers, no one could consistently beat this game.

After my blackjack session I rejoin my son and find that he's won 50 pesos in the slot machines. He always was a lucky kid.

Toward the end of my trip, I fly to Bariloche on the north end of Patagonia, where some Nazi war criminals supposedly escaped to from Germany at the end of the war. There is even a rumor that Adolf Hitler and Eva Braun lived there after faking their suicides in Berlin.

On the flight, I pick up the airline magazine, which is published in both Spanish and English. I read the Spanish first and then check the English translation to find out how I did. I'm pleased to find that I'm beginning to comprehend a lot more Spanish. One of the articles, reprinted from *Newsweek*, is called "Buff Your Brain," by Sharon Begley. She writes that the best thing for your brain is to learn a second language. "When a brain that is fluent in two languages chooses between, say, English and French, the cortical circuits that hold both languages become active. The prefrontal cortex must then step in to choose the right word—man or *homme*?—for the circumstances. The prefrontal is also the site of those higher-order functions. The workout it gets in bilingualism carries over, buffing such IQ skills as problem solving and attention switching."

When the article begins discussing short-term memory skills, which it refers to as the brain's "scratch pad," it says that "short-term memory may be the foundation of pure intelligence to a greater extent than anyone suspected." It describes an exercise conducted by Susanne Jaeggi of the University of Michigan where volunteers heard a string of letters while seeing a series of computer screens with a blue square that appeared in different places. They had to identify when the spoken letter or the square's position matched that of several screens earlier. This required both attention switching—from auditory to visual cues— combined with remembering rapidly changing information for short periods of time. This sounds a lot like card counting: verbally interacting with dealers while remembering constantly changing information—the flow of the cards—and using the result to make betting decisions. But the best part is yet to come. Scientists speculate that learning these skills improves the "purest form of brain power, fluid intelligence—the ability to reason and solve problems independently of existing knowledge."

How nice, I think, *that card counting might not just be the pursuit of easy money and the subversion of the casino system; it might also make me a more intelligent person.*

I've often wondered what it is about Bill—more specifically, Bill's brain—that makes him such a rock-star card counter. Thus far, he has seemed rather uninterested in analyzing the question. For him it's a given, like being tall or having good eyesight. He'll sometimes lightly say, "Yeah, I've always been pretty good at math." Or, "I've noticed I could memorize phone numbers easily." But card counting isn't so much raw memorization, or even mathematical calculations. Card counting is about rapidly assimilating abstract information in a highly distracting setting. As I read Begley's article, I make a mental note to press Bill for more information on this subject when I see him next.

Arriving in Patagonia, at the Bariloche Airport, I'm picked up by a handsome, middle-aged shuttle driver with ruddy cheeks and a deep voice. He speaks little English, so I ask him in Spanish if he likes the Hyundai minivan he is driving. He replies with a passion-ate affirmative and soon we are comparing notes about what cars are popular in America versus Argentina. I may appear calm as I do this, but I'm privately high-fiving myself for carrying on a conver-sation in Spanish. After we're done with cars, we talk about fishing and hiking with equal success.

As I watch the fall landscape glide by, my guide describing the local trout streams, I have a slight stirring deep inside that I am making progress toward at least one of my goals: speaking a second language. As for my second goal on this trip, counting cards, I know I've improved somewhat, but I need a reality check in a casino. At this point, that possibility seems quite distant.

After I'm dropped off and settle into my hotel, I head out for a quick walk around town in the late afternoon. I've heard about the Andes my entire life and I'm dying to see them with my own eyes. Just the name *Andes* seems so exotic. But it's a cold afternoon and the wind is howling, whipping up waves in Nahuel Huapi Lake. At the end of the lake, backlit by the sun, distant and hazy, are the jagged peaks I've come to see. I can't wait to rent a car tomorrow and explore.

As I walk back through town, blackjack is the furthest thing from my mind. But low and behold, I see they have a small casino on the main street. I enter and, on a brief walk-through, I see the tables have no continuous-shuffling machines—a good sign. It's a beautiful little casino and it feels so different from those in Las Vegas. For a moment I wonder why. Then it hits me: they actually have windows. Casinos in America are notorious for having no windows (so you don't think about leaving) and no clocks (so you don't know how long you've been playing). Furthermore, the layout of casinos has always seemed intentionally confusing.

Later, I do a little research on this subject and find an interesting article posted on InformalScience.org (http://archive.informalscience. org/researches/VSA-a0a6d2-a_5730.pdf) by Stephen Bitgood, professor of psychology at Jacksonville State University. Bitgood contrasts the layout of casinos to those of shopping areas and museums. He says designers purposely make casinos easy to enter but hard to leave. They align the casino floor at an angle to the street outside. On the casino floor, there are no right-angle intersections, no "you are here" maps, and no landmarks other than gambling areas. He concludes: "They intentionally attempt to confuse people in the casino areas by reversing design principles in an attempt to increase time (and therefore, money) spent. However, the principles of good orientation design are applied in shopping areas in order to facilitate more efficient shopping. It's all about money!"

Here in Argentina, they evidently haven't reached this level of deception. In fact, I could sit and play blackjack while gazing out the large windows at the stunning Nahuel Huapi Lake. However, the tables are empty at this hour, draped in cloth, and no dealers are in sight. In Spanish, I ask a security guard when the tables open up, and he tells me the action begins at eight o'clock each night.

The next day, for my tour of the Lake District, as they call this area of Patagonia, I rent a two-door Fiat with a 1.2-liter engine and a five-speed manual shift. It has no power steering, no power windows, and no automatic anything. But the little car is fun to drive, and it sips gas (which they call "nafta" here). In an email, I had told Bill that I expected Patagonia to be the most beautiful place on earth. It is spectacular, and it has huge lakes that remind me of Montana's Glacier National Park.

Back in Bariloche, I have time to nap and then warm up my brain by counting down a few decks in my hotel room. I get the sensation that my brain is a muscle that is warming up, getting ready for exercise. I imagine different areas of my brain lighting up as the cards fly past my eyes. I'm nowhere near as fast as Bill, who can scan and count a table of cards in one glance, but I've really increased the speed that I can count through a deck. I head out and walk through the dark, windy streets to the casino feeling excited and nervous.

I time my entrance to the casino right at eight o'clock, hoping to play alone against the dealer. I walk in and find three tables opening up. I sit at one and watch a pretty young woman in a checked vest and white shirt, stripping the plastic off six decks of new cards and spreading them on the table. She silently begins "washing" the cards, spreading them randomly to make sure they aren't clumped together. In some cases, sharp-eyed blackjack players look for these clumps and use a technique called "shuffle tracking." They try to remember sequences of face cards from the previous shoe, which they call "slugs," and raise their bets accordingly. This ritualistic washing breaks these clusters of cards apart and makes the shuffles more random. The dealer divides the six decks into even stacks and shuffles them expertly, the cards making a crisp riffling sound on the padded felt. Finally she looks up.

"Juego?" she asks in Spanish. Loosely translated, *juego* means "game." She is inviting me to place my bet.

I've cashed in with only 200 pesos, but I get a nice pile of real, thick casino chips, not like the chintzy plastic ones I practice with. The table minimum is only 10 pesos, but I play two hands against the dealer and put two chips on each hand to start with, the way Bill taught me. I win both of the first hands and get a couple of blackjacks in the first shoe. Whenever I get 21, the dealer calls out "*Black-a-jack!*" in English but with an Argentine accent.

I find I still can't actually count cards, but I watch for a flood of low cards so I'll know when to raise my bets. With 20 pesos on each hand, I split a pair of 8s and then double on one of my split hands. The other hand is a double too and the dealer busts, so I win them all. I have so many chips I actually ask for *cambio*, or change, because I don't know how they say "color me up" in Spanish. As I play, another woman is watching, an older one, who I assume is a pit boss. It makes me wonder if a casino this small has an Eye in the Sky. I search the ceiling for the dark plastic domes that hide the camera lenses. I see nothing.

The second shoe isn't quite as good, but I still make some money. I don't want to get on the other side of the bell curve, so I decide to cash out. I find that I've doubled my money and I only played a half hour. I turn in my chips at the cashier's cage and leave. Outside, the cool air feels good and I spend some of my new pesos on a bottle of Argentine Malbec from Mendoza. It's a tip of my sombrero to Bill and his Vegas ritual where he buys a bottle of good wine in the Bellagio with *their* money. As I walk back to my hotel, I'm mildly encouraged.

The next day, I have what is probably my best conversation in Spanish. I go into a store on the main street to buy a belt made of *carpincho* leather. I'm alone in the store with a young man who is very friendly and talkative. After we get the details of the belt ironed out, we chat about other things. I tell him my son lives in Buenos Aires and is studying architecture. He replies that his father is a professor of architecture and has created many of the designs in the city. We talk for nearly fifteen minutes and I understand most of what he says. As I leave his shop, I'm walking lightly, feeling as if my goal has been accomplished. I didn't really learn Spanish, but I saw what it would take to become fluent. And I felt that, given time, I could do it.

That afternoon I catch a bus back to Buenos Aires. As I pass the casino, and recall my win from last night, I feel a powerful urge to play again. With another month of practice, maybe I'll actually count cards, rather than just look for a flock of low cards as a signal to raise my bets.

Later, on the bus, I sit and watch the countryside glide by. My Argentina trip is coming to an end but I still have three months left on my sabbatical. That should give me enough time to practice card counting and make a few runs at the casinos in San Diego or go back to Las Vegas. But then it occurs to me: I could take that old Lexus project car, and drive it across the country, stopping at casinos as I go. I could even swing by Bill's house in the Midwest and we could hit his local casinos for a tune-up. As I think about the trip, I visualize a map of the US with a zigzag line of my progress from one casino to the next. I even allow myself to visualize dollar signs on the map next to the casinos to show all the money I'll make. How much could I make if I played every day? A grand? Two grand? I've seen Bill do that in one quick session. Now, it's my turn.

Chapter 8

Scouting the Indian Casinos

"We're eating for free while you're skinning the casinos!"
— My eighty-six-year-old father

Early one morning, about a month after returning from Argentina, I set off for the Indian casinos in the mountains north of San Diego along with my father, who is visiting from Massachusetts. My cross-country blackjack trip will start in a few weeks, and I'm eager to get as much practice card counting as I can before I head out. I've printed out a list of addresses for the casinos; my father is going to be my navigator. He's in fine spirits because he's up early in the morning, and he's on a mission. I can almost feel his happiness radiating from the seat next to me as I drive south through rush-hour traffic.

My father, eighty-six, has begun visiting me in California more frequently since my mother died two years ago. While she was extraordinarily healthy for most of her life, she developed congestive heart failure, declined over a two-month period, and died at home with all of us around her. Since then, my dad has seemed lost and the balance of the family has shifted. It's become obvious that it was my mother who held us all together.

Driving through the early morning mist of Southern California, heading for the casinos, I can't help wondering what my mother would think of our little adventure. Actually, I know exactly what she would think. She'd absolutely hate it. Not only was she deeply religious, she was also a Depression-era child with ultraconservative views of money. It's amazing—yet somehow wonderful—that at my age, I still worry about my mother's opinion.

We arrive at the Pechanga Resort and Casino in Temecula, which is nearly across the street from the city's high school. Each morning, as the kids head to class, they see lines of cars pulling into the huge parking lots around the lavishly decorated hotel and casino. Meanwhile, they stumble into classrooms hearing the mantra that a good education, and hard work, is essential for success—which I agree with, by the way. But I can't help thinking about the mixed message sent to the younger generation when they see the rising popularity of casino gambling and state lotteries.

We hoof it into the casino and find it deserted. It's still only 8 a.m. I leave my father among the slot machines and walk around looking for what Bill would call a good game. I was hoping for a tune-up on a nice little $10 single-deck game. But the best I can find is a two-deck game with a $25 minimum.

Suddenly nervous, I take $300 out of my pocket with a pounding heart and lay it on the green felt.

After the young Asian American dealer—Alex, according to his nametag—finishes shuffling, I watch carefully as he places the yellow plastic cut card close to the middle of the two decks. Bells go off in my head and I hear Bill's voice say: "This is *not* a good game!" The penetration is nearly 50 percent rather than the hoped-for 25 percent from the end of the decks. But I decide, "What the hell, I'll play one shoe and then get out before the damage is too great."

As I place my two chips on each betting circle, I am ashamed to see my hands are still shaking. I'm only glad that Bill isn't here to see it. But then I watch in amazement and relief as I win both my first hands—an immediate boost of $100.

"Good start," Alex mumbles. He looks almost as nervous as I am, and I wonder, briefly, if he went to the high school across the street. He deals the next two hands. I win them too, and the next, and the next. In fact, in that first shoe, I win nearly every hand and even win two doubles. I'm almost feeling a little greedy and smile benevolently as he wins the last hand. When I cash out I find that I've turned my $300 buy-in into $685 in less than ten minutes.

Alex colors me up, turning my stack of greens into blacks, and I go to the cashier's cage carrying my chips, feeling their weight in my hands, recalling the times I was jealous of Bill's wins in Las Vegas. I savor the moment as the cashier pulls out a stack of bills, snaps them crisply, and counts out a long row of $100 bills followed by a trickle of twenties and a five.

"Dad, check this out," I say when I locate my father seated at a slot machine. "I just won $385." I fan out the money in front of his face, as if he might not believe me.

"Oh boy!" he says, standing up. "And I just won thirty bucks in the slots!"

I'm amazed at the power of the casino to quickly turn my East Coast, professorial father into a happy-go-lucky gambler. He's even saying "slots" now rather than slot machines. I'm just hoping he doesn't start searching for the "loosest slots," as some casinos promise. It's an awful phrase designed to create a mixture of sexual desire and greed that is as crude and effective as a Karl Rove campaign slur. But suddenly, life is good—I've got a pocket full of dough, and my dad won just enough to cover his lunch.

Back in the sunlight, we enjoy the drive to the next casino. The road winds down the valley, under outstretched branches of live oaks that dapple the sunlight. As I drive, I think back to how my hands were shaking when I laid out my chips. This is a testimony to the power money holds over me. I'm sure I'm not unusual in this regard, but it still surprises me. Sometimes it seems that money is the most real thing in the world.

The richest person I ever met was Allen Funt, the creator of the TV show *Candid Camera*, whose biography, *Candidly, Allen Funt*, I wrote in the early 1990s. Once, he told me he was worth $25 million. At the time, I was nothing more than a struggling freelance writer with a young family and big dreams, so his vast fortune impressed the hell out of me.

Often, Funt would speculate about how much of an advance we might receive for the publication of his biography. I didn't say anything, but I wanted to ask: "Why the hell do you care? You've already got more money than you or any of your children or grandchildren could ever spend in a lifetime!" Then I realized that it wasn't the *having* of money that he desired but the *getting* of the money. When the money went from someone else's possession to his, there was a semisexual thrill of the transfer, the flow, if you will, which turned him on.

This is the gambler's high, the feeling of those chips leaving the dealer's tray and coming over to your side of the table. And I was just as hooked on that feeling as anyone else. I didn't *need* the money, but I certainly *wanted* the money. That's why I was willing to suppress my normal aversion to risk and lay my $100 bills on the table. It's what kept me dealing blackjack hands at the kitchen table, playing computer blackjack, reading strategy books, and bombarding Bill with constant questions.

After another few minutes of driving, we approach a casino located up a narrow road between neatly plowed fields. This casino is actually in an inflatable tentlike structure similar to the ones they use back East for indoor tennis courts. But inside, it's the same old thing: darkness, flashing lights, pounding music, and acres of slot machines. Today, there is a slot machine tournament, and dozens of senior citizens are furiously jabbing at the machines and screaming in excitement. How the hell can someone win a slot machine tournament? Apparently, they win if they just hit the "spin" button faster than anyone else. The spectacle of hyped-up seniors focused on this menial task is both alarming and depressing.

The blackjack game here looks good, but after just one shoe, in which I lose $15, another couple joins me. I decide to move on. When I reconnect with my dad he has won even more in the slots. His mood can only be described as euphoric.

We push on to our final stop of the day, the appropriately named Valley View Casino, perched on top of a hill overlooking the wine country north of San Diego. I feel the amazing clash between the natural beauty of the area, and the hideous disregard the architect—assuming there even was one—had for meshing this design with this landscape. It looks like the entire structure was lowered from the sky by an alien spacecraft.

Inside, I'm amazed to find an open table with a $10 single-deck game. On the green felt, the rules state that a blackjack pays only six to five instead of the customary three to two. Later, when I relate this to Bill, he says, "That's not a good game at all. It really cuts into your profits. You shouldn't have played it."

The trend toward the six-to-five payout began around 2003 and has been spreading ever since. Although it seems like only a small reduction of a player's winnings, experts calculate that it makes a big dent in a player's bankroll. In the *Las Vegas Sun*, writer Jeff Haney says that a blackjack player using basic strategy and betting $10 a hand will lose an average of about $1.80 an hour playing a good single-deck game. "At a game that pays six to five for blackjacks, however, our hero can expect to lose more than $14 an hour. In other words, he will lose his money at least five times more quickly at a six to five than at an old-fashioned single-deck game."

The *Sun* quotes UNLV professor Bill Thompson as theorizing that six-to-five blackjack rode into Las Vegas on the same wave as topless swimming pools and sexy pirate shows on the Strip. "Maybe the casinos think that everyone coming to Las Vegas is thinking below the belt instead of with their brains," Thompson says.

I wish I had known about these poor odds in six-to-five games at the time. Instead, I decide I need the practice and, after my earlier $385 win, I'm gaining confidence. I buy in with $300 and the dealer, named Rick, pushes a stack of chips across to me. He's a hip, middle-aged dude with shoulder-length hair, bobbed like a woman's, and sleek, dark-framed glasses that he is forever taking off and then putting back on. He's like a TV soap opera doctor who pauses dramatically, takes off his glasses, and then delivers some fatal diagnosis.

Playing head-up against the dealer, I lose $300 in about fifteen minutes. I drop down to one hand just to try to stop the bleeding. Still, I lose. I feel my shoulders sagging and my stomach has the hollow feel of a big (for me) loss. But then I remember a conversation I'd had with Bill recently.

"Do you think confidence has much to do with winning blackjack?" I asked him.

"No question about it," Bill answered. "If you're not confident, you're beat before you even sit down at the table."

"But if it's all about math, why should that help?"

He paused and answered carefully. "There are some intangibles in this game that I can't explain." He was quiet for a moment, then added, "They say that in life, you should think positively. That holds true for blackjack too."

"But aren't we just back to talking about luck then?"

"Not the way casual gamblers talk about it," he said. "To them, it's all luck. To us, it's confidence and knowing that the mathematically correct play will eventually get the right result. That's the knowledge that gives you confidence."

Thinking of Bill's quiet voice, filled with confidence and certainty, gives me a "What Would Bill Do?" moment. I picture him sitting here, chatting casually with the other players, pretending to be discouraged when the dealer draws to a 21, or high-fiving on a successful double-down to maintain his novice image. He would, I conclude, eat this game—and its shitty odds—alive.

I square my shoulders and take another $100 from my pocket and throw it on the table. As the dealer counts out more chips for me, I do one more thing: I smile. It is my version of the wink that Bill gave me in Las Vegas the first time I saw him play. I've used it in tennis when I'm receiving a serve in a close match. It sends a signal back through my nervous system that if I'm smiling, I must be more relaxed, more confident than I thought. And when my opponent looks across the net, he can't help but wonder, *What the hell is he smiling about? What does he know that I don't?*

Something magical begins to happen. The cards slowly begin to fall in my favor. Gradually, I win back a lot of money. In fact, I win so much that I finally relax enough to realize how hungry I am. My stomach feels like a knotted fist, tensed for a fight. So I break for lunch. I tell the pit boss I'm willing to get a players' card so I can get a comp for the buffet. I pocket my chips, look around, and find my dad sitting nearby at an empty table reading on his iPad. We find the buffet and then cash in my comp. Dad buys his own lunch with his winnings from the slot machines. When we get our trays, and check out the food, Dad is a kid in a candy shop.

"Boy oh boy, look at all this food!" he exclaims. Then, as he begins scooping hefty portions of nearly everything, he belts out, "We're eating a free lunch—while you're skinning the casinos!"

"Jeez, Dad. Keep it down."

"But you are! This is the best buffet I've ever seen. And it's free! Free!"

They should have videotaped my dad and used it for an advertisement for this casino. Of course, my dad never met a buffet he didn't like. Whichever buffet he is currently eating at is the best buffet he's ever seen.

As we settle down to eat with heaping plates of food, my dad announces that in the dessert section of the buffet there were fourteen different types of fudge. I'm counting cards, and he's counting fudge. Something for everyone, I guess.

Returning to the blackjack table, I find I have company. I'm sitting next to an elderly man who doesn't seem to speak English but is enjoying himself enormously, betting tall stacks of green chips with wild abandon. When he runs out of chips, he opens a wallet as thick as a phone book and stuffed with $100 bills. With a wistful smile, he pulls out a sheaf of hundreds and buys in for another grand.

Suddenly, he hits a 16 and gets 5 for 21 and a big win.

"Nice hit, Papa," comes a voice from behind us.

I turn to see a middle-aged man in Bermuda shorts holding a paper coffee cup. This is the first of a running string of comments from this kibitzer, all addressed to "Papa." It's not unusual to have spectators who are too scared to play but want to participate as cheer-leaders hover behind blackjack tables. At first I find these comments annoying. But then I realize it's a good test of my concentration. And besides that, Papa and I are now winning, so I decide to roll with it. It's easy to have a good attitude when the chips are coming your way.

Soon, we get a change of dealers, and here comes Reggie, a tall, thin African American guy whom I like immediately. He cracks his knuckles and announces to the table, "Okay, let's make some money for these nice folks."

And he does. But something even more remarkable happens. Now that some of the fear of losing has been erased, I relax enough to focus. And I begin, for the first time, to actually count cards at a real blackjack table. Since it is a single-deck game, there are only about four hands dealt before the reshuffle and a new round begins. So I don't have to keep the count for a long time. I only have to look for which of the four hands, if any, has a high count. When I see lots of low cards coming out on the first hand or two, I know there's a good chance the last two hands will be favorable. So I spread my bets, raising from $25 to $50 and, several times when the count is higher, to $75.

It's slowgoing and my count isn't perfect. Also, the cards are dealt facedown, so I have to be alert for the moment when the cards are flipped faceup as the dealer rakes them into the discard tray. Still, my counting pays off and I build up a nice stack of chips. Eventually, I draw almost even, erasing my loss, and I cash out with a $300 profit for the day.

In the parking lot, I text Bill: "Won $300 in Indian casinos in San Diego. I counted cards for the first time."

I get an answer back from Bill almost immediately. "Counting works, doesn't it?"

"No doubt," I text, and fire up my car.

Before I pull away, I hear the chime from my iPhone and see I have another text from Bill. He writes: "I'm proud of you."

These kind words, from a tough teacher, are the biggest win of the day.

For my dad, the trip has also been a great success, except that he ate too much at the buffet. He naps peacefully much of the way home as I let my mind drift. I'm psyched that I actually counted cards, and I can't stop thinking about where this could lead. I feel like casinos are ATMs where I can go and make a withdrawal any time I want. I know I'm getting ahead of myself; I still need to prove that I can sustain this kind of success on my upcoming cross-country odyssey. But with a successful session of actual card counting under my belt, I'm eager to get going.

Part Two:
Coast-to-Coast Blackjack

Chapter 9

The Extraterrestrial Highway

"There are three subjects you can count upon
a man to lie about: sex, gas mileage, and gambling."
—R. A. Rosenbaum

There's a little town on the Nevada-Utah border where they've got single-deck games you can beat like a drum," Bill tells me by phone while we discuss my route across the country.

The plan is for me to take a $3,000 bankroll and play as much as I can on my way from Long Beach, California, to my family in Boston and back again. I'll also stop in the Midwest and see Bill for a few days to get a checkup on my card-counting progress. I'll be driving the teal green 1996 Lexus ES 300 project car. We want to show that the old guy (the car, not me) can make it coast-to-coast without breaking down. But also, the trip will double as my blackjack tour of the US.

"The town is technically called West Wendover, but most card-counting folks call it Wendover," Bill continues. "It's a pit, really—just one street with five or six casinos. But the rules are great. So you can play one game, pick up your coffee, and walk to the next casino. Buy in for maybe $300 and leave when you've doubled your money. You can make a quick grand there. Then, when you reach the end of the street, cash out and get the hell out of Dodge."

I look on Google Maps and find that Wendover is 640 miles away, a good ten-hour drive from my home in Long Beach. Not exactly on my way. But the idea of starting my trip with an extra grand in my bankroll is indeed attractive. I also love the Wild West sound to it: *When you reach the end of the street, cash out and get the hell out of Dodge.* It makes me feel like I'm a roving gambler, a modern-day Wild Bill Hickok . . . except for the part where he is shot to death while playing poker in Deadwood, South Dakota.

Later, I tell my son Tony where I'm going, and he tells me that comedian Louis Black called Wendover, "one of the three best places to go if you're thinking of killing yourself." He adds that the locals have given it the nickname "Bendover." A quick web search shows that the town's population doubled between 1990 and 2010 as the casinos moved in. It's safe to assume that, because it's only 123 miles from Salt Lake City, more than a few Mormons have snuck across the border for a little unsanctioned fun. Interestingly, its counterpart across the state line, Wendover, Utah, is shriveling up economically because, with no casinos, it has little tax base.

Ever since my win in San Diego I've had something I wanted to ask Bill about, and now seems like a good time. But I find that I'm a little self-conscious about raising the subject. So I bring it up in a sideways fashion.

"I keep thinking that I could hit Vegas and the Indian casinos once a month," I say to Bill.

"Yeah . . ." he responds, waiting for more.

"Of course, this is if I really improve," I say. "But my thought is this: if I created a circuit, and worked it carefully, it might be pretty decent money. It might almost be enough to live on."

"I know where you're going with this," Bill says. "You want to be a pro."

"Well, all I'm saying is that it's crossed my mind," I say, backpedaling now.

At first I feel foolish, like I might get slapped down. Instead, he surprises me.

"You could do it," he says. "I mean, if I wanted to, I could make a hundred and fifty grand a year."

"That's more than I make now," I say. "But how many hours a week is that?"

"It's not the hours at the table," he says. "It's the travel, and being away from home. But you—you've got some very good games in your backyard. You're a four-hour drive from Vegas. And you've got those Indian casinos all around you."

So now my trip has another component to it: it could be the beginning of a new career. Could I really become a professional blackjack player? I'm sure many have started down this road before. But what turned them back?

The night before I leave on my trip I realize there is still one piece of business I need to take care of. I take out a fat envelope from my bureau sock drawer. Inside is my bankroll of $3,000, all in $100 bills. I look at the pile of cash and try to imagine it growing and what it might look like when I get back from my cross-country trip. I write the amount in the envelope, as well as the date, on the outside of the envelope and head out to the old Lexus.

An old car like this won't attract much attention. Still, I have to be careful since, obviously, people going into casinos usually have a lot of money with them and are vulnerable to stickups. Where would a car thief look for hidden cash? I admit, I'm being a little over-dramatic, but I enjoy the intrigue. And it reminds me of a story Bill told me about how he won $18,000 in Las Vegas one weekend shortly after 9/11. He headed to the airport with wads of money stuffed in all his pockets and his carry-on luggage just hoping it wouldn't be detected by the scanners. He says some blackjack players, who travel with more than $10,000, carry a signed letter from their attorney, stating they are professional gamblers and not terrorist money launderers.

I open the trunk and pull up the old, stained carpet liner. Under that is a layer of foam insulation with a coating of adhesive that gives way easily. I slip the envelope underneath the insulation, smooth it back in place, and replace the trunk liner.

I'm ready to go.

The next morning I have breakfast with my family, say good-bye, and head north. It's Sunday morning and the road from Los Angeles to Las Vegas is jammed with traffic coming the other way. *Watching someone else's misfortune always puts you in a good mood*, I think as I roll along. I imagine most of the people heading south are tired, hungover, and light in the wallet. But I feel superior because I'm heading north with an old car, a full tank of gas, and a fat bankroll hidden in the trunk of my car.

It's weird to drive through Las Vegas and not stop. I can feel the casinos exerting a gravitational pull on me. But I keep my foot firmly on the accelerator and, about twenty miles north of Las Vegas, I take Highway 93 north through the sun-blasted, desolate landscape. After another fifty miles I come to the junction with Nevada State Route 395, where a cluster of vehicles is parked near a grove of towering cottonwood trees. People are milling around, so out of curiosity I stop and look at what they are all inspecting. It's a sign reading "Extraterrestrial Highway" and it's plastered with graffiti and stickers for rock bands and various political causes. I chat with a family from England who knowingly inform me that farther down the road is the Air Force's top-secret "Area 51," where they are keeping a couple of aliens in a deep freeze. The family assumes I'm headed in that direction. No, I tell them, my destination will provide a different type of encounter altogether.

It's a fitting start to my journey.

The rest of the day I spend driving along Nevada Highway 93, which snakes through long green valleys with grazing cattle, groves of cottonwood trees, and a string of small towns. I even pass a brothel, which is open for business and has a crowded parking lot—a sight I've never seen before. My destination is the town of Ely, pronounced "Ee-lee" by the locals. I plan to stay there for the night and then push on to Wendover in the morning, early enough to beat the crowds and play the single-deck games. I climb up and over a high mountain pass and then descend into the little town. Casinos line the main street, although they have only slot machines. In the center of town is the old Nevada Hotel with a huge neon sign of a crazed prospector swinging a pick ax. This hotel, once the tallest building in the state, would now be lost among the towering and equally bizarre casinos on the current Las Vegas Strip. I park and head for the entrance.

As I push through the casino door I am overwhelmed by the sense that I am in the wrong place. First, there is the smell that hits you at the door of every casino: cigarette smoke soaked into old carpets. For me this is such an evocative smell, a smell of a different time, of my childhood, when they allowed smoking anywhere, without a thought for the health effects. But now, it is a smell you only occasionally get when you walk into a casino.

The next impression when entering all casinos is the sound—the ringing bells from slot machines, the pounding music, and the excited screams of craps shooters. And finally, there are the flashing lights from the strings of bulbs hanging everywhere, desperately trying to lure you into some crazy game of chance. It is all a potent package designed to pump up your fun factor, to convince you that you are having, or will soon have, the best time of your life. And that money will be pouring from every slot machine in sight.

I had read that there are blackjack tables here at the Nevada Hotel. So I wander around among slot machines looking for the action. Finally, I find a sign saying the poker and blackjack tables are in the basement. I find the stairs and descend into a dank, undecorated basement that could have been used to film the killer's lair in *Silence of the Lambs.* Turning a corner I see two bartenders leaning on their elbows on a tabletop watching me enter. At a single blackjack table, with a $3 minimum sign on it, slouch three farmers in baseball caps with plastic beer cups in front of them. A husky female dealer, who looks like she drives an 18-wheeler in her spare time, jokes with the players as she tosses out a steady stream of cards. I give the game a wide berth but they spot me, smell fresh meat, and one of them drunkenly calls out, "Come on 'n' join the game!"

"I'm going to get something to eat first," I say, retreating quickly. "But I'll be back."

I hurry upstairs and try to brace myself for the basement experience by eating a tuna melt with sweet potato fries. But as I chew and consider the situation, something occurs to me: I just can't go back down those stairs. There is no earthly reason to join that game. So I return to the Lexus and drive out of Ely, probably never to return. The sunset is gorgeous, a fan of reds and oranges spreading across the sky in what my son, when he was little, described as "God beams." The sight is made so much sweeter by the relief at not being in that basement of horror, at that depressing blackjack table.

Soon, it's dark, and the moon rises. Checking the mileage on my GPS I see I must be close to Wendover and, sure enough, coming up over a rise, I see a strip of lights in the distance. I feel like a cowboy on horseback, riding in off the range after months of isolation. Even from here, I could see white-hot searchlights probing the night sky and the bright pillars of individual casinos, like shrines to the great god of luck.

I pull into town and see a gaudy sign, a three-story cowboy waving and saying howdy. Along the main street are five casinos, each with a different theme. It's obvious that Wendover is a Las Vegas wannabe. People walk the sidewalks carrying drinks, wandering restlessly from one casino to the next. I'm so tired after my day of driving I need to get settled soon. At random I pull into the parking lot at the Peppermill Casino and Hotel and step out into the hot, dry desert night.

I get a room for $79 and find myself in an outsized Roman-themed room, with ankle-deep carpet. I didn't know they had shag carpeting in Rome. The air-conditioning is cranked up so high they could hang meat in here. I unpack, wash my face, and go back down to the casino for a quick walk around to help me prepare for tomorrow morning's assault.

Sure enough, there are plenty of single-deck games, but nearly every seat is taken by rowdy, leather-vested, beer-drinking bikers. It looks like my favorite scene from the 1985 film *Pee-Wee's Big Adventure*, where he stumbles into a biker hangout and wins them over by doing a bizarre dance to "Tequila" on the bar. As I pass one blackjack table I hear a biker shout, "Gimme a little card . . . Come on, little card . . . YES!" This is followed by cheers from his biker buddies as they all live out what could be an advertisement for casino fun.

Back in my Roman sanctum I enjoy the solitude. I deal out a few hands of blackjack and feel my tired brain trying to keep up with the count. The results of my practice session are negative and leave me feeling nervous about tomorrow.

Surprisingly, I sleep well and I'm ready for the tables after a quick shower and a cup of coffee. I count out two stacks of money, each with $500, put them in separate pants pockets, and head down to the casino. It is vastly transformed from the Bacchanalian festivities of last night. The expansive room is nearly vacant. The blackjack tables are empty. Only a few seniors are grazing among the slot machines, staring at the spinning numbers while sipping coffee from paper cups.

I find a single-deck game where a white-haired dealer named Daniel with thick glasses waits patiently. I sit down and put $300 on the table.

"Good morning," I say pleasantly. "Did you just start or have you been here all night?"

The dealer begins to count out my chips. "Been here since three."

"What's it like here at that hour?"

"Some players are just gettin' their groove on," he notes philosophically. I have my chips and I'm ready to go. He pats the table. "Good luck, sir."

I push two red chips onto each betting circle for a whopping opening bet of $20. Daniel deals the cards facedown in what they call a "pitch game." According to casino rules, you can only touch the cards with one hand, to prevent cheating, no doubt. I awkwardly struggle to corral the cards, pick them up, and my sleepy eyes focus on a welcome sight: blackjack. *Nice.* Daniel is a slow dealer, which matches the speed of my foggy brain. But I whip my thoughts into action and begin keeping the count. I find the count is shooting up after only the first hand or two. My count isn't perfect but it's a pretty clear indication of when the cards are in my favor. As Bill predicted, these are perfect playing conditions.

Ten minutes later another guy joins me so I cash out and find that I've won $175. It's a modest but encouraging win. I visit the bathroom and write this information on an index card, so I can track my winnings and also remember when I played at each casino. It is the system Bill taught me and I have found it to be essential. In the excitement of rushing from one casino to the next, and playing different sessions, it's surprisingly easy to forget where you stand.

I buy another coffee and walk across the street to the Rainbow Casino. It's still early morning and the air is cool but the strength of the sun foreshadows the heat of the day. I step from the blazing morning light into the timeless gloom of the casino. The Rainbow is more upscale, even though it's actually owned by the Peppermill. It's even bigger, with an interesting addition to its decorations: large illuminated pictures of outdoor scenes. There might be, say, a picture of a Vermont meadow with cows grazing. Then, as you look, Bossy raises her head, still chewing, and looks at you. It's startling since it's not a static picture—it's a looped computer scene. But I can't help wondering what prompted them to include these pictures here in a casino. Did someone think it would keep the gamblers inside even longer since now they had no reason to go out and explore the natural world? There's just so much I don't understand about casino management.

I approach a heavyset dealer at a one-deck game with kinky salt-and-pepper hair who reminds me of my seventh grade biology teacher, Mr. Regan. I buy in for $300 and begin winning almost immediately. The dealer, Mr. Regan, goes from friendly to frosty and I can't figure out why. At one point, with the count shooting up, I triple my bets. He pauses and cocks his head as he looks at the sudden increase of chips. Finally he says, "Okay . . ." very slowly, and continues dealing. I get a double and win.

Then it hits me. He is letting me know *that he knows* I'm counting cards. Bill told me these one-deck games are vulnerable and the casinos are nervous about card counters. But it's not up to the dealers to do anything about it. In the old days, casinos hired dealers who could cheat card counters out of their winnings. Now, it's up to the Eye in the Sky, and the surveillance experts, to decide when a counter is a threat and should be backed off.

I decide not to push my luck and I tell him I'm cashing out. When I ask him to color me up, he assesses my win of $340.

"Nice," he says with an edge in his voice. "You doubled your money."

He pushes a small stack of chips back to me. I'm about to ask where all my money went when I see that I have reached another milestone in my blackjack career: he paid me with a beautiful purple $500 chip and an assortment of black, green, and red chips. I'm getting back my buy-in of $300 plus the $340 I won, for a total of $640.

I go to several other casinos, but by now it's getting busy and the tables are filling up. I return to my Roman villa and pack up as I wait for the shift change that is coming at 11 a.m. Bill has told me that it's important to know when the shift changes are made because then you get to play against a new crop of dealers, pit bosses, and surveillance personnel who don't recognize you. Also, at 11 a.m., they often open more tables. Hopefully, I can sit down and have a quick session before another player joins me. Before I head back to the action I decide I should change my appearance and pull on a new shirt and a nondescript old baseball cap. I flatter myself thinking I'm actually getting good enough to be a threat.

I wind up back at the Rainbow and see several dealers hanging around drinking coffee and waiting to start their shifts. Killing time, I loiter among the slot machines and on an impulse, put a dollar in one of them. Three and a half bars come up and I win $3. I'm having a good day.

After the shift change I find that the dealer who looked like my biology teacher has been replaced by a doughy young woman with a thick rope of strawberry blond hair down her back. She isn't interested in me, my witty banter, being in this casino, or dealing cards. I accept the apathetic silence and buy in for $300. I lose $100 immediately. This is to be expected after so much good luck, I think.

A middle-aged woman joins the table, spilling two lonely chips onto the felt. I decide to keep playing just for practice. A short time later the woman's daughter joins us too. I can't imagine gambling with my mother. In fact, I probably wouldn't be playing at all if my mother was even still alive. But this mother-daughter team keeps asking the dealer whether they should hit or stand and what cards they should split. I wonder why they are throwing money on the table if they are reduced to asking the dealer for advice. Even a cursory glance through any blackjack book would give them the top seven basic strategy rules that would cut their losses drastically. In fact, casino gift stores sell basic strategy cards you are welcome to take to the table with you.

There are over 270 basic strategy moves, and I am still struggling to learn some of them, particularly what to do with the "soft doubles," those hands that include an ace. Since the ace can be either 11 or 1, it provides a big advantage and often prompts an opportunity to double down. For example, an ace plus either 2 or 3 doubles against a dealer's 5 or 6, while an ace plus either 4 or 5 doubles against a dealer's 4, 5, or 6. It doesn't sound hard, but you have to remember this in the heat of the moment, with money on the line, keep the count, and laugh at the dealer's jokes, too. Basic strategy has to be reflex so you can concentrate on the count.

The basic strategy plays I keep forgetting I eventually write on index cards and keep in the car. Several times a day, while I'm driving, I quiz myself to relieve the boredom and look forward to winning more hands when these uncommon card combinations come up.

This woman's repeated request for advice from dealers is not uncommon and not altogether illogical. I see it happen all the time at the blackjack tables. The dealer stands there day after day seeing the cards flow, so they should be an expert on the subject, right? But, Bill is quick to point out, they are not.

"You know more than the dealers," Bill tells me. "In fact, you know more than the pit bosses too. You might even know more than the casino managers. What they know is the stuff that gets passed around, back and forth, and was never true in the first place."

Sometimes, if Bill is getting heat from a pit boss, he'll pretend to need advice and will point to his cards and say, "Should I hit or stand?" The pit boss will give his opinion and if it's right, Bill makes the recommended play. If not, he says, "You know, I think I'll play a hunch," and makes the play that the count dictates. Either way, it helps make it look like he's not a card counter.

Meanwhile, this middle-aged woman is frozen over 17 against the dealer's ace.

"That's what I call the mother-in-law's hand," the dealer says, coming alive for the first time. I sense a punch line coming. "You want to hit it but you can't." The mother-and-daughter team howls with laughter. Then the mother decides to stand on the 17 and loses as the dealer flips over a 9 to go with her ace.

Meanwhile, I get an ace, 7, and because of my basic strategy flash cards, realize I should double it against the dealer's 5. I win the double and my stack of red chips grows even taller, with some green chips to give it class. Soon, I've erased my $100 loss and my profits are growing. I feel like my counting has really improved. And I wish Bill was here so I could say, "Look! My hands aren't shaking!"

I love it when I raise my bets and then get face cards and aces. And I find I'm almost pleased when I reduce my bets and lose. It's like ducking a punch and watching it sail by, unharmed.

The daughter jealously eyes my stack of chips. "Look at *him*," she says. "Look how much he's winning."

"I bought in with $300," I tell her, feeling suddenly exposed. "Most of this is just my own money."

"Yeah, right. How much have you got there?"

"He's got $520," the suddenly talkative dealer answers. I feel as if someone just revealed my yearly salary to my underpaid officemates. I decide it's time to bring this session to an end.

Giddy and almost in shock, I realize I am within one more win of netting the grand that Bill predicted. After a short walk back to the Peppermill, during which I almost shrivel up in the blasting sunlight, I find the only table open has a $10 minimum instead of the $5 tables I've been playing. I decide I am ready for the big time. I buy in with $300 and face a middle-aged dealer with dyed hair whipped into a froth of curls. She is bubbly and talkative until I begin to win, which I do almost immediately. After fifteen minutes someone else sits down so I tell my now sulky dealer I am leaving.

"Yeah, it's a good time for you to get out of Dodge," the dealer observes.

I am startled by her choice of words since it is almost exactly what Bill said to me on the phone last week. I tip her $5 and she mutters an icy thank-you. I assume she has realized I'm counting cards. These two hostile dealers I've encountered make me feel like a real pro. I'm even hoping that I can get backed off someday. Then I'd really feel like I'd arrived.

Back in the Lexus, with the AC on max, I spill out all the bills from my pockets. It's a merry jumble of hundreds, twenties, tens, and fives. I feel wealthier than ever before in my life. It's so much fun to separate the piles and see a thick stack of $100 bills. My win for the day is $940. And that's for only about two hours at the tables. It's like I discovered a money tree and did little more than pick off the bills.

I hop on the interstate and cross the line into Utah. Soon, I'm flying across the Bonneville Salt Flats, which I've never seen before. I try to focus on the stark beauty of this natural phenomenon. But all I want to do is review the intoxicating and highly addictive feeling of winning money. Then it occurs to me that my euphoria is, in part, because I've experienced the first glimmerings of what it is like to feel smart. Of course, huge measures of luck *are* involved here, so I try not to get ahead of myself. But it shows me what a powerful goal I've set for myself by using card counting as a measure of my intelligence. And now my pockets are stuffed with bills that prove some success. I feel like I might be able to join a tiny, elite group—people who actually win money in casinos.

But two days later, recalling this happy time, I realize that on some level of my mind, there was a subtle warning note, a little voice saying, "It just can't be this easy."

Chapter 10

On the Road

"As I picked up my winnings and left, I noticed an odd mixture of anger and awe on the dealer's face. It was as though she had peeked for a brief moment through a familiar door, into a familiar room and, maybe, she had glimpsed something strange and impossible."

—Edward O. Thorp, *Beat the Dealer*

Early the next morning I roll across Wyoming with the peaks of Rocky Mountain National Park in the distance to the south. Along the way, I see a surreal vision—a forest of giant, ghostly white electricity-generating windmills, with blades as big as the wings of a 747, turning slowly in the prairie wind. I've seen several of these wind farms recently and it is one of the encouraging positive changes I see taking place in our country on my cross-continent drive.

On the negative side of change is the alarming number of casinos sprouting up everywhere, like venomous weeds ready to trap the unwary. I imagine that in the boardrooms of penthouse offices the mega-rich are saying to each other, "Put all your money in casinos, boys! You can't lose!" Certainly, the casino business has been a boon for magnate and conservative political contributor Sheldon Adelson, worth a cool $23 billion in 2011. Of course, to make his casinos profitable he first had to break the unions that represented the workers that helped him make his fortune. Now, he's using his vast wealth to alter the course of America by donating to Republican Super PACs.

Obviously, I'm conflicted about this subject of casinos. I believe that with Bill's help, I can get in and out and win money—most of the time. But the vast majority of players at the blackjack tables, and at the baccarat, craps, and roulette tables, and everyone at the slot machines, are losing money. Yes, losing, losing, losing. Yet, people don't seem to realize the damage they do to themselves. Or they don't care. Or they simply can't control themselves.

This resignation to losing is almost universal among gamblers. Once, I was on a packed elevator with Bill returning to a casino parking garage. There was a heavy silence in the elevator until Bill called out, "So, did we all win?" There was a collective groan from everyone, a groan that could be interpreted as, "You've got to be kidding me!" The groan was followed by a thunderclap of understanding laughter. Here is the duality of the gambler's mind: *I might win!* This is the thought that brings someone to a casino. The thought as they leave is, *Of course I lost again.*

Bill told me his elderly aunt always sets aside $700 for the slots whenever she goes to Las Vegas with her friends. Once, he offered to take her money and use it as a bankroll at the blackjack tables.

"Okay," she said. "You can have part of the profits if you win. But the losses are yours."

Bill laughed. "What the hell kind of deal is that?"

"Take it or leave it," she said. He left the deal and she continued to blow the money on slots.

I spend the rest of my day's drive crossing Nebraska. Late in the afternoon, I'm restless and bored and call a reservation clerk in a Council Bluffs, Iowa, hotel. The clerk tells me, "You can't miss the hotel—it's right off the interstate near all those new casinos."

It's a jolt to my system. *Did she somehow know who she was talking to?* I file this information away in my memory, but I can feel the excited expectation of a playing session growing in my system. After I check into my motel, I head out to scout the casinos with $1,000 in my pockets.

That day I had talked to Bill on the phone and reviewed what to look for in a "good game." Once again, Bill puts deep penetration at the head of the list in choosing a good game.

"But what if there is no penetration notch to show you how many cards they cut out?" I ask Bill.

"Some dealers don't even know how much it changes the odds. So buy in, wait until they shuffle, and see where they put the card. If penetration is bad don't put out any bets. Just say, 'You know what? I'm going to play a different game.' It's your money and you have to protect it. Even one hand could be a $50 loss you don't need. That's the cost of a dinner."

I think of this advice as I pull into the parking lot of the brand-new Horseshoe Casino in Council Bluffs. The enormous parking lot is nearly full, and on this pleasant evening, people are streaming into the entrance, which is rimmed with gaudy flashing white lights. Inside I find mostly eight-deck games, many with automatic shuffling machines. Besides that, there isn't an empty table in sight. I scout two more casinos, including a Harrah's, and find similar rules.
I return to my hotel and have a good night's sleep.

The next day I'm driving when Bill calls. I'll be at his house tomorrow night, so we confirm the time and directions.

"I've been thinking," Bill says. "When you get here I want to show you a new count."

My brain is just beginning to wrap itself around the Knock Out system and feels like there isn't any room for more information. But a great teacher will always be one step ahead of you and stretch your mind to the limit. Besides, if I am going to make a living at this I need the best count available.

"Is that the Hi-Opt 1?" I ask, thinking it is a count I read about in a blackjack book.

"No. It's the Zen count," he says. How appropriate. I'll learn the Zen count from the Zen Master. He continues: "It's so accurate you will basically know when you are going to get a blackjack. So, that way you can have your big bets out there when the high cards are coming."

I like the sound of that. But what he says next really gets my attention. "With this count you'll win more money and you'll win it faster."

My reaction to that is: I want to learn this count and I want to learn it now. But I also don't want to spend a long time out of the action learning anything new since I've had some nice success lately.

While we're talking I see an exit sign for the Prairie Meadows Casino, outside Des Moines, where they supposedly have a single-deck game. I say good-bye to Bill and exit the interstate.

It's a cool, breezy morning as I step out of the Lexus into a parking lot dotted with only a few cars. Looks promising. Inside, I take an escalator up to the second floor, which, unlike most other casinos, is not smoky or jammed with frantic gamblers. Instead, it's oddly pleasant and relaxed. Neatly dressed dealers stand invitingly behind racks stuffed with chips. I want those chips. And I feel confident about getting them. But Bill's words are still echoing in my mind: *you'll win more money and you'll win it faster.* Too bad I don't know this new count yet.

I find a single-deck game and buy in with $300. The dealer is a young woman with dirty blond hair and a friendly, uncomplicated, Midwestern face. We chat as she shuffles, but I see that, uh-oh, here they actually use a cut card to eliminate the bottom third of the deck. In Wendover and at the El Cortez, they deal a set number of hands before reshuffling. Even worse, according to the rules on the table, blackjacks pay only six to five. I ignore this warning signal since I'm still feeling invincible from my wins in Wendover.

The game begins and I don't win a single hand on the first shoe. Since I want to play two hands against the dealer, the casino requires me to double my bets, so my chips disappear at an alarming rate. It's as if some large vacuum hose came down from the ceiling and just sucked them up. I'm doing my best to keep the count, but it's always negative and the cards I'm getting are just terrible. Panic sets in. Halfway through the second shoe, and a raft of more losing hands for me, this nice schoolteacher of a dealer is literally wincing as she gives herself a steady stream of aces and picture cards.

All too quickly, I'm flat out of chips. I feel like I've been slugged in the stomach and I'm gasping for air. But I recover my nerve and pull another $100 out of my pocket. I figure any wild swing in one direction will have a sudden swing in the other direction. Not so. My next hundred disappears at the same steady rate. The dealers change, but my luck doesn't. By now, any thought of counting cards is gone and I'm just hanging on by my fingernails, hoping that simple basic strategy somehow saves my ass. I'm down to the last few chips when I get a double. I don't have anything to double with so I pull the last $10 bill from my wallet and double with that. And lose.

Stunned, I stand there looking at the place my chips used to be. I croak something about getting more money from my car and stumble back through the casino and out into the parking lot, a total of $480 lighter. The envelope in the Lexus is still stuffed with cash and I think about getting some more money and trying to turn my game around. But in my heart I know that's not the right thing to do. Besides, I recall Bill once saying, "Sometimes you need to get some cold air on your face and back away for a while." I decide to do just that.

Back in the car, I feel like I've been in a fight and I don't know how badly I'm hurt. Did I break a tooth? Cut my face? In a similar fashion I check my psyche for injuries. Actually, I find I'm okay. It is still a beautiful June day. Birds are singing. I have gas in the tank and places to go. I begin to feel better. If this is going to be a permanent addition to my life I'll have to learn to take these losses.

I take solace in the idea that at the very least, I'm hoping to get a good book out of this. I'm in territory that few people like me have been in. I'd never be here if it wasn't for Bill. And I know I will be seeing him tomorrow night.

During the afternoon, when I need a break from driving, I stop in rest areas and take out my bag of poker chips and playing cards. Sitting at concrete picnic tables, I deal myself blackjack hands and find I rarely lose five hands in a row. In a few cases I'm down only $50 after the first shoe. So how did I get clobbered so badly in the casino? I decide it was an anomaly.

Pulling into Joliet, Illinois, an hour later, I see a sign advertising the Hollywood Casino. I follow a winding road through a beautiful forest of tall hardwood trees. I've left the Great Plains behind me and this now looks much more like the East. It's so tranquil here along this country road that I can't imagine it leads to a casino. It's more fitting for an entry to a cemetery. But, sure enough, I come around the corner and see a grandiose casino situated on the banks of the Des Plaines River. As I get out in the parking structure, I see that some of the guest rooms are actually on a riverboat. I tell myself that after a nice win I'll try to score a comp and stay here.

Inside, it looks like a lot of people hurried here right after work. Construction workers wear grimy jeans while business men and women are still sporting formal office-wear. The joint is jumping. However, I find an open two-deck game with a $25 minimum. As I sit down and lay $300 on the table, the young, inexperienced-looking dealer shuffles and puts the cut card three-quarters of the way through the decks. Good penetration. Payoff for blackjack is three to two and double after split is allowed. Everything is looking good.

Except for the cards I get.

It's not the slaughter I experienced in Council Bluffs, but I'm bleeding to death in a steady series of paper cuts. Not only that, but a gangly hillbilly with a sleeveless shirt, who looks like a meth addict, keeps trying to join the game in the middle of the shoe despite signs that clearly state this is not allowed. This breaks my concentration and I lose the count—not that it would matter much, since I can't put together two cards that total higher than 15. Meanwhile, every up card the dealer gives himself is a picture card or an ace.

This time, I don't decide to try any heroics by pulling out more money. I idiotically tell the dealer to "have a nice evening," tuck my tail between my legs, and leave. Being a dealer must be like being a traffic cop; most of the time, you just go around ruining everyone's day. I walk back through the casino in a state of shock, totaling the loss for the day at $780, nearly wiping out my win in Wendover.

I'm in the mood for some serious self-flagellation, so I drive back toward the interstate and check into the cheapest, most disgusting hotel I can find. The place I find certainly fits the bill: the registration process takes forever since the check-in clerk is completely incompetent; the room I get looks like the set for a '70s slasher film, the bedsheets were last used for an orgy and weren't changed, and the TV is one of the last tube models left in the State of Illinois.

I can't stand being in this room.

There's plenty of daylight left, and it's a warm spring morning, so I go looking for a golf course to hit some balls. I pull into a course next to a city park. As I step out of the car I see I'm surrounded by tall elms, which reminds me of being a kid and visiting my relatives in the North Shore Chicago suburbs. I remember the buzzing locusts and the hot summer stillness among the big trees. Back then my grandfather was my hero because he knew the home plate umpire for the Cubs and got us free tickets to home games.

I go into the pro shop to buy a small bucket of golf balls from the young man behind the counter. His accent is so thick it's like talking to John Belushi in *The Blues Brothers*. I get another wave of memories, this time of my early years working as a police reporter for the City News Bureau of Chicago.

As I head to the practice tee, it's dusk and I discover that the mosquitoes are out now, flying in attack squadrons. Living in California we don't have to worry about such annoyances—only earthquakes, wildfires, and riots. I also discover that somewhere between Long Beach and Illinois my swing has developed a nasty slice, alternating with the occasional shank. I set out to cure my swing but only succeed in nearly kneecapping the guy next to me with a hosel rocket. I retire to a local pizza joint, sit at the bar, and watch the Cubs game. They are losing, of course.

That night when I talk to my wife, my beautiful, trusting wife, she asks if I "had any casino action today." She was dubious of this whole undertaking, but she was impressed with my wins in San Diego and Wendover. I can tell she's hoping for more good news. I just can't face telling her of my big drop. Instead, I bite my tongue and say that I just scoped out a few casinos, not mentioning the loss at all. I rationalize that I'll tell her the bad news once I can soften it with more good news.

Then it hits me—the denial I criticize other gamblers for is now in my repertoire. Next time I'm in a casino, and see one of those signs that say, *Does someone you know have a gambling problem?* I better call the number myself.

Chapter 11

Inside the Zen Mind

Q: "What's the difference between a person who prays in
church and someone who prays in a casino?"
A: "The person who prays in the casino means it."
—Joke on the wall of the Gambler's Bookshop in Las Vegas

'm weaving through late afternoon rush-hour traffic,
heading for Bill's house, when I look down and see the temper-
ature gauge in the old Lexus is climbing. Luckily, my el-cheapo
GPS unit shows I'm only about six miles from Bill's house.

I pull off the highway and find a parking lot for a quick inspection.
Under the hood, I immediately locate the problem: a steady stream
of coolant is pouring out the rear of the engine. There's nothing I can
do here, so I slam the hood shut and jump back behind the wheel.
I push on toward Bill's house with one eye on the road and one eye
on the temp gauge. I wind through a maze of suburban streets listening to my GPS calling out the turns. A hundred yards from my
destination the needle pegs itself on high.

But now I see Bill standing outside his house waving, a wide smile on his face, looking very casual in plaid Bermuda shorts and a white golf shirt. He beckons me into the driveway but I park at the curb, not wanting to leave a slimy puddle under my ailing car. I climb out and he shakes my hand warmly. It's great to see him and, because it's been a while since I've seen him, I'm struck anew by his presence: his broad, rugged face, his friendly yet probing eyes. And of course, his soft, strong voice.

I explain my predicament with the overheating engine and Bill commiserates.

"Wow," he says. "And that just happened?"

"It started heating up just after I made it through the city."

After I say this, I mentally recap all the desolate stretches of road I'd driven through where it would have been a nightmare to be stranded. I see various scenes from my trip like a burst of short movie shots in a horror film—the two-lane road in Nevada, the vast expanses of prairie in Wyoming and Nebraska, or my journey through any one of many cities.

Bill nods, smiling, reading my thoughts. "Man, that was pretty lucky."

"Sure was."

Luck is a loaded word for Bill and me. Gamblers use it constantly to describe hot streaks that strike without warning and evaporate in an instant. Gamblers pray to the great god of luck and invoke its powers with talismans and elaborate rituals. But Bill doesn't go there. He puts his trust in mathematics and prays in church, not in the casino. Still, some events defy explanation and even the odds. Like my overheating car. There are about twenty-two hundred miles of road between my house and Bill's. The car overheated in this final six-mile stretch.

This overheating incident triggers a strange thought. The events of our lives are so infinite they really can't be predicted by anyone but God. The events in blackjack are finite, and with card counting, the outcome can be predicted (assuming you play long enough and have a big bankroll). Maybe that's why the game is so addictive: I can exert a modicum of control on a complex game in a world seemingly ruled by chaos and random interaction.

We go into Bill's neat, spacious home and grab a beer before dinner. We are chatting about the trip when Bill's wife, Pat, arrives. I've sensed from Bill that their marriage is very strong, so I've been looking forward to meeting her. A retired schoolteacher who now tutors underperforming students, Pat is very pretty, tall, and blond, with a sharp Michigan accent.

After dinner, Bill and I go down to his finished basement for a blackjack tune-up. He takes out two decks of cards and some poker chips and he begins explaining the Zen count. Developed by British blackjack expert and author Arnold Snyder, the Zen is a multilevel counting system. Unlike the KO system that assigns a plus or minus of only 1 to the cards, the Zen assigns plus 1 and 2, and negative 1 and 2 to the key cards. Bill takes a small square of paper and, in his exacting handwriting style that makes me think of the precision with which he plays blackjack, he writes the values for all the cards. Later, I carry that slip of paper with my bankroll for good luck. Yes, you see, I'm not above speculating on the mysterious effects of luck occasionally.

"Let me show you how it works," Bill says, shuffling a deck of cards and pushing a second deck toward me. I shuffle them and we combine the decks.

Bill deals a few hands, showing me how he adds 2, 3, 7 as plus 1 and 4, 5, 6, as plus 2, while 8 and 9 don't affect the count at all. The ten cards are all negative 2 and the ace is negative 1. Bill stops after dealing two hands of 3, 7 and 3, 9.

"See, the Zen shows me it's time to raise my bets now. But the KO still has you flat betting."

"Wait," I say, amazed. "You mean you've been keeping two counts at the same time?"

"Well, yeah," Bill shrugs.

"Where do you put them?"

"What do you mean?"

"In your head. Where are the numbers?"

"I don't know. But when I need them, the numbers are there."

"And you don't forget them in between hands?"

"No. Never."

I envision one of those old-time calendars that flip over the numbers for the different days of the week. They use that technique in old movies to show the passage of time. If I could look into Bill's head, I imagine I would see those numbers flipping over at different rates.

"It also helps to use an ace side count," he continues.

"What's that?"

"You count the aces as they're played and keep track of them separately."

"Okay, wait," I say, laughing. "So you can keep two completely different counts and then you also keep an ace side count?"

"Yeah, but the ace count isn't really a *count*. I do it in letters: A, B, C, and so on."

"Oh sure," I say. "That makes it so much easier."

Now I picture Bill's mind as if it is an engine house on a ship. Little men in white jumpsuits monitor rapidly changing dials showing the count and the number of aces. Then, when these little men see the dials hit the right level they shout into speaking tubes: "Raise your bets! Attention! Raise your bets!"

Meanwhile, I struggle to keep a single number in my brain.

Bill isn't particularly interested in discussing how his brain works, just that it does work. He's very focused and directs my attention back to the cards.

"Okay, the count is high now and we've only seen two aces. In a two-deck game there are eight aces so probability will tell you we'll get them in one of the next two hands."

He flips over the cards and gets a blackjack.

"There you go," he says, patting the cards with the back of his hand, one of his interesting little mannerisms. "This count is very accurate at predicting blackjacks. Sometimes you'll get two in a row—boom, boom. You want to have your maximum bets down when that happens."

"I wish I'd had this system at Prairie Meadows," I say. "Maybe I wouldn't have gotten stomped by the dealer."

"Actually," he says. "What you need to do is make better use of your indexes."

He's referring to index plays that change basic strategy when the count is either very high or very low. I'd read about index numbers but never tried to use them. I was still struggling just to remember basic strategy and keep the count.

"You really think index plays could have helped?"

"Hell yeah. It tells you when to hit on a 12 versus a dealer's 4, 5, or 6. Since the count is low, that means the next card will be small enough so you won't bust. And if the count is high, you want to stand on a 15 or 16 because you know the next card is going to be a 10 and it will bust you. For the MIT team we used eighteen different indexes. For you, you might only use the top four indexes, which would cover about 80 percent of your needs. That, and knowing when to take insurance, gives you a huge advantage."

Insurance is offered by the dealer when her up card is an ace. With an ace showing, there is a chance the down card is a ten, which gives her blackjack. By putting out an additional bet, half of the original bet, you can take insurance. If the dealer has blackjack you don't lose whatever you've bet. In most cases, insurance is considered a sucker bet. But when the count is high, Bill says taking insurance is the single best play you can make and it can save you a ton of money.

Thinking back to yesterday's losses, it would have been nice to have fought back with these strategy changes rather than just sit there and get annihilated by the dealer.

"The other thing you could have done yesterday is to change the rotation of the cards," Bill says.

"How?"

"Whenever you make a different play, all the cards that follow are then different. So, for example, you can drop down to one hand when the count is negative. Then the sequencing of all the cards that follow is different."

It's a mind-blowing concept. The alteration of only one card transforms a session from a disaster to a bonanza. I can't help but relate this statement to life. It's like saying that if you leave your house for work just one minute later in the morning, then you miss that fatal accident on the freeway that had your number on it. Such are the consequences of our decisions.

Conversely, the good luck we experience is often the result of fluky decisions too. For example, I met a young woman while going to the University of North Carolina in Chapel Hill but never got to know her. Two years later, I bumped into her by chance on the University of Chicago campus when I first moved to Chicago. We began seeing each other, got married, had two sons, and now we've been together for over thirty years. Where would I be today if she had taken a different route that day? Or if, for a moment, I had looked the other way and just missed her?

Bill puts away the cards and pours me a glass of red wine.

"There's something else I wanted to talk to you about," he says, sipping the wine.

"What's that?"

"When you're at the table, you have to stop thinking of the chips as money."

I know instantly what he means. But just as quickly I decide this is impossible. He studies my face and sees I'm rejecting this.

"Seriously, it's essential."

"Why?"

"If you look down at the table and see you have a chance for a double or a split, but that will mean laying out $200, you can't say to yourself, 'But that's a day's pay!' You just need to make the bet."

"So what do you do?"

"You think of the math—the reason you're doubling, or splitting, is because you have a good chance of winning more money."

I must not look completely convinced. So Bill continues.

"A couple of months ago, I was in Las Vegas with Pat. I was down a grand or so and she couldn't watch so she decided to take a walk. All of a sudden, the count went through the roof so I put $250 on each hand. I got two 7s on one hand and an 11 on the other. The dealer showed a six, which was a perfect bust card. I split the 7s and doubled the 11. The dealer gave me a 7 and I split it again. Then I got another 7 and I split again. On one of the 7s I got a 4 for another 11 so I doubled that too. I had to keep reaching into my pocket for more money. All this was taking a long time to play so a crowd was forming behind the table.

"Finally, I had five hands with two doubles for a total of $1,750. But I knew what I had to do and I did it. The thing is, you don't get this kind of a chance very often so I couldn't back off. It was funny because, when Pat got back, she found a huge crowd at the table.

Bill sips his wine.

"So what happened?"

"What?"

"With the hand—did you win?"

"The dealer's hole card was a 10 for 16. Then she drew a 6 to bust."

"Nice."

"Yeah, it brought me all the way back."

I loved hearing stories like this. There was something seductive about the sound of all of that money.

"So you have to make the right decisions mathematically speaking, not change your playing because you've decided it is too much money. Just know that the law of probability is on your side; you're probably going to win. And if you don't win this time, you'll win the next two times."

I do my best to look convinced. But I can't stop thinking of what it would feel like to put that much money on each hand. As usual, my face reveals my feelings. Bill finishes his wine and stands up.

"You'll see," he says. "We'll play tomorrow and you'll see. And we'll get that money back that you lost at that crappy game in Iowa."

Chapter 12

Gambling Fever

―――――――――――――

"When the problems began, I convinced myself that one more bet would solve everything. But one bet led to another, leaving me with the pain of lost money, lost time, lost self-respect, and the pain of losing control."
—"When the Fun Stops," a Nevada Council on Problem Gambling pamphlet, found in Las Vegas casinos

We arrive at the Horseshoe Casino in Toledo late on a Friday afternoon and it's a complete madhouse. Cars are streaming into the parking garage and, inside, people are rushing through the doors with that expectant look on their faces, filled with pent-up Friday night energy that means they want to cut loose. And, in this case, cutting loose is drinking and gambling.

"Sometimes, when a casino just opens, they offer favorable rules just for a promotion," Bill says, his intense eyes scanning the vast casino floor as we walk through the door. Music is pounding, bells are ringing, and somewhere, someone is screaming for joy. It makes me think how I once heard that casinos pipe in the sound of slot machines paying off to create the feeling that winners are all around you. Your turn is next!

Pat and I are trying to keep up with Bill as he circles the pits, muttering in disapproval.

"Hit on soft 17 . . ." he says to no one in particular as he reads the rules of the different games. "Eight decks . . . No double after split . . . Automatic shufflers . . . Why does anyone play these crappy games?" He shakes his head in disgust.

"Isn't there anything here worth playing?" I ask hopefully. I've been looking forward to seeing Bill play. Now that my own skill level has increased I want to see the Zen Master in action to improve my game even more.

"Nothing," Bill's face is a storm cloud. "I'm not going to throw my money away on these crappy games. Come on. Let's get out of here."

I'm a little disappointed that we can't play, but I'm also a bit relieved. After the beating I took in Des Moines and Joliet, I'm still gun-shy. Bill must sense this and wants to get me back to the table as soon as possible.

It's late and we haven't eaten anything. As we head back to the car, Pat remembers that there's a local restaurant that's supposed to be really good, with the very Toledo-sounding name Tony Packo. I Google the directions on my iPhone and soon we are weaving through a warehouse district by the river. We pull up in front of an unassuming red clapboard building and as soon as we walk through the door I know I'm going to love this place. The menu is mainly hot dogs and their homemade beer. The most popular item on the menu is fried pickles.

We sit in a noisy dining room with the late evening sun slanting through the window, illuminating the dust in the air. The beer is excellent, and after only half a mug, I know I'm going to want another. But Bill tells me we might head back toward his city and visit his stomping ground and play in the casinos there.

"They have a fabulous two-deck game," he says, taking a thirsty swig of his amber brew. "I'll play it and then maybe you can give it a shot."

The nervousness begins building. And when the waitress comes around, I decline a second round.

As we drive back from Toledo, Bill talks about his early days playing blackjack. The stories come easily and are filled with details of different counts he was using and even some hands he played that brought big payoffs. What he doesn't talk about much is himself and his feelings. It's as if he doesn't really think that's very interesting. And yet, I sense there is a lot going on inside, a lot of backstory that would be fascinating if I could just open him up.

Once, during one of our phone calls, I bring up the topic of his reticence.

"You don't really talk much about yourself," I say, trying to provide an opening for Bill. My comment is met with silence.

"Is that true?" I press. "You don't like talking about yourself?"

After a long, awkward pause Bill finally answers: "I don't know what you want me to say."

I think about his response and then begin to laugh. "Well, I guess that kind of proves it, doesn't it?" I say. "You don't feel comfortable talking about yourself."

Now he's laughing too. "Look, I'll tell you anything you want."

"Sure, I know that. But I just don't think you know how interesting it all could be."

"All what?"

"Your thoughts, insights, feelings."

Another long silence.

"Okay," he finally says.

The most extreme demonstration of Bill's sometimes terse answers came when we were sharing a pizza in Las Vegas a few months after I met him. My wife had pressed me to ask Bill about people who had gambling problems and lost more than they could afford. She wanted readers of my book to know the dangers of gambling as well as the thrills. Our conversation went something like this.

Me: *Have you known people who had bad gambling problems?*

Bill: *Oh sure.*

Me: *Can you think of an example?*

Bill: *A friend of mine had a big problem.*

Me: (after waiting for him to elaborate) *How big of a problem?*

Bill: *Lost his house.*

Lost his house! Yes, that is a big problem. But there were no details offered about who the friend was or how he could have lost his house. Bill isn't interested in that. He's interested in winning at blackjack.

During the drive back to Bill's city, Pat seems to sense that I am only getting the tip of the iceberg so she fills in some of the details. And between the two of them, I get a sketch of Bill's early years.

Bill's family was from a small Christian town in Lebanon called Manara. His father, who spoke four languages, moved the family to Colombia, in South America, to open a business. But when they got there his mother hated it because it was very hot and she thought it was a poor environment for her children. Bill was the youngest of five. The business Bill's father started was successful, but at night he would go to the local casino and blow his money playing baccarat and roulette. This made his mother furious.

When Bill was only five, his mother died under mysterious circumstances, perhaps because of poor medical treatment by local doctors. His father decided to pull up roots again and they moved to the US to join Bill's uncle in the Midwest. His father went on ahead and Bill, at the age of seven, entered the country with his sisters through Miami. Alone and unable to speak the language, they boarded a Greyhound bus for the trip north.

Living in the US, gambling continued to be a problem for Bill's father. "He was always blowing our money in a poker game in someone's basement," Bill recalls with bitterness.

Bill picked up English quickly while going to school. And in high school he played football and baseball. Later, he went to Eastern Michigan University, before transferring to Wayne State University, where he married his first wife and had two daughters. He began his career as a teacher, but after only a few years he got laid off and began selling insurance. He divorced and remained single for several years. One night he met Pat at a Bible study meeting. They went out for coffee, began dating, and eventually got married.

Bill downplays the difficulties of his childhood. But Pat tells me, "Bill basically raised himself. He's a survivor. He was always protecting his sisters. And now he's taking care of his father."

Sitting in the backseat of the car, watching the cornfields of the Midwest roll past on this late spring evening, I think of all the unusual events of Bill's life that led him to this point. And still, I sense there is more, much more, to tell. While I haven't really figured out what makes him tick, at least for now, I'll settle for this outline of his life.

A few hours later, we're walking into the casino where Bill cut his teeth. It was here that he first played nearly fifteen years ago after work one day with some friends from his office. Bill brought about $80 and lost it all in a few minutes. "This is stupid," Bill thought. All his friends lost too.

"How do you play this game?" Bill asked.

"Well," his friends told him. "They have these little cards in the gift shop that teach you something called 'basic strategy.'"

Bill bought one of the cards and then began doing some additional research. He came across the book *Knock-Out Blackjack*, which had just been published. He read it and remembered being intrigued. He practiced each day, and within four months he could count down a deck of cards in eighteen seconds. That meant he could flip the cards over, either adding or subtracting 1 for each significant card. In the KO count it is plus 1 for 2, 3, 4, 5, 6, 7 and minus 1 for 10s and aces.

About six months after Bill's first foray into casino play, he returned and, counting cards, won $750. Ecstatic, he told his co-workers about his victory.

"Aw, you just got lucky," was their response. "That happens sometimes. But in the long run, you'll lose."

Bill returned to the casino a week later and won $500. Now his friends were listening. A short time later, Bill's weekly wins were averaging much higher amounts.

"After a while, they might as well have just written me a check for a thousand bucks and left it in an envelope at the door," Bill recalls. That's why he doesn't play at his local casino very often. He knows they have their eye on him. When he comes with a friend, he has that person get a card under their name and then he uses it. The only problem then is he has to remember who he is supposed to be so he can respond if the pit boss addresses him. At many casinos he has learned to respond to the name Pat, which is his wife's name. She often gets him cards under her maiden name to hide the connection to Bill.

When Bill first started playing at his local casinos, in the rough sections of the city, the other people at his table were pretty colorful. After winning a big hand, some of them would jump up and celebrate their victory by dancing around the table. In other cases, fine white powder covered the bills they pulled from their pockets and threw on the table—probably cocaine or heroin. They got the bills from a big drug deal and were celebrating with a visit to the casino.

Now, it's homecoming night, I think, as we walk into his casino. And I can see Bill is itching to play. He's no different than a golfer who's been away from the links too long, or any tennis player who hasn't smashed that round yellow ball for a while. It's his sport, and he's ready to get his mojo on.

We settle down at a six-deck, $25 minimum table. Bill buys in with $500 and the game begins. Almost immediately a young woman sits down at our table with a small stack of chips and a drink.

"Do you mind waiting for the end of the shoe?" Bill asks, not taking his eyes off the cards.

"Till the end of *that*?" she says, indicating all the cards left in the six-deck shoe.

Bill doesn't answer. On the next round she pushes her chips into the betting circles anyway. It's as if she can't stop her hands from gambling. Bill gathers up his chips and we move to another table.

This is a six-deck game with a $50 minimum, so it's unlikely anyone else will barge in. Right away the vibes at this new table are better. Bill begins playing two hands against the dealer and I can finally relax and enjoy the show.

When I first saw Bill play, I didn't know enough about this game to fully appreciate his skill. But now that I've had a number of my own sessions, I know what he's doing, as well as why and how tough it is to do it. What strikes me is the effortlessness of his performance, both mentally and physically. There's the matter of what's going on in his head: keeping the count, adjusting it for the number of cards remaining in the deck, and sizing his bets—all the while keeping an eye peeled for casino heat. Then there is his graceful table play, his elegantly simple hand signals, the way he guides the chips from one pile to the next with the nudge of a little finger, and the instant but unhurried doubles and splits. Bill does all this with rock-steady hands, not like my pathetically quivering fingers that spill chips and flutter the bills as I draw them from my wallet.

The dealer must sense that Bill is an expert because he matches Bill's rhythm, and the two play off after each other, building a nice skyscraper of chips. Overall, it's like dance performed to percussion instruments: the snap of the cards and the rattle of the chips accompanied by the low hum of comments from Bill and the dealer as the cards fly. It's as if Bill has tapped into some energy stream where he exerts control over numbers and tames the nasty deviations this game dishes out to the unwary. For this blazing streak of wins, Bill is in control.

Pat and I watch, mesmerized.

I see that Bill is confidently spreading his bets from the $25 table minimum to $75 and then $100 on two hands. The dealer gives Bill a 10 against his 6 up card. Bill doubles. On the other hand he splits a pair of 6s and now he has $300 on the table—not really that much for Bill, given his background of $30,000 hands when he played with the MIT team. But it's enough to catch the attention of the Eye in the Sky. The dealer flips over his down card and has a 9. He hits and gets a 7 and busts by one. Bill rakes in a total of $600 in chips.

Bill seems to be in complete control and the chips at his side show how much damage he's doing to the casino. I'm so engrossed in the game, almost chuckling with delight at his success, that at first I don't hear the intercom. The second time it sinks in.

"Paging security," the voice says. "Security to the high-limit area."

Out of the corner of my eye I see two white-shirted guards hurrying toward us. They pass our table and take up a position in Bill's eyeline, arms folded across their chests. I look at Bill's bets and see he's cooling it—only $50 on each hand. A moment later, a young woman in a formal black dress, the casino manager, appears next to the table.

"Nice evening, isn't it?" she says to us.

If I was in mid-sip of my drink, I would have spit it across the table like in a corny sitcom. Her comment is ridiculous and absurd on so many levels. First of all, how does she know it's a nice evening? Casinos are the ultimate anti-natural location, divorced from time, space, and weather. So how, exactly, did she know it was a beautiful evening and why was she telling us this in the middle of trying to play cards? It's not like we're strolling around outside, taking in the night air. Also, the comment is unconnected to anything. You don't walk up to someone focusing intensely on a task and say, "Excuse me, it's a nice evening, isn't it?"

But Bill must know this is just a way to try to break his concentration and let him know that they know what he's doing. He finishes the shoe and stands up.

"Okay, I'm done," he says, a little irritated. He gathers up the chips and we head to the cage.

"I didn't want to push it," he says, almost apologetically. "I want to be able to come back and take more cash later."

Of course, I'm crassly focusing on the results. I try to sound casual as I ask, "How much did you make?"

"Eight hundred," Bill says, his voice flat. I've heard that tone of voice before. Last time we were in Vegas, and he won *only* $460, he yawned and said it was, "Like kissing your sister."

We're moving toward the exit now.

"Sorry you can't play," Bill says. "I think we shouldn't be seen together right now."

"I can wait," I say, trying to keep the relief out of my voice.

Bill hardly even looks as the cashier counts out his money. He folds the stack of $100 bills and tucks it away.

"We'll come back tomorrow, or try the casino across the street. They have a good two-deck game."

Bill walked in a half an hour ago. And now he's walking out $800 richer. Despite the biography I'd gotten, I'd say he's a little more than a survivor.

Chapter 13

My Lucky Day

"I remember that casino fondly: the courtesy and the hospitality, the spacious, attractive modern dining room with its fine cuisine, and the casino with its juicy little cluster of blackjack tables, the favorable rules, and last, but not least, the free money."
—Edward O. Thorp, *Beat the Dealer*

The next day we are walking off the golf course when my phone rings. I see by the number that it is the dealership where I left my car to have the overheating problem fixed. I've done lots of stories for my company's website about service department upsells and rip-offs, so I brace myself before answering. The worst part is I don't have any negotiating leverage; I need the car fixed and I need it fixed today.

"Mr. Reed?" the service advisor asks.

"Yes," I answer, steeling myself for an argument.

"Your car's all fixed. You can come and pick it up any time."

"Fixed? You mean it's all fixed." I repeat inanely. Usually, they call with an estimate first, you throw out half the items, settle on the work to be done, and negotiate the price. Instead, they're just saying it's fixed. I don't know how to deal with that.

"It turned out that it was a loose hose clamp at the back of the engine so we just tightened it up." This is too good to be true. "Oh, but we did find one thing."

Uh-oh, here it comes . . .

"The radiator cap wasn't holding pressure so we replaced it. But that's only going to set you back $19 so we went ahead and took care of it."

I thank him profusely and disconnect, feeling lighter than air. I had braced myself for a $200-plus bill and instead it was a cheerful $19.

Two hours later, I'm still feeling relieved about my car. And, after a shower and some lunch, Bill, Pat, and I walk into the MGM Casino in the downtown section of Bill's city. I can tell by Bill's attitude that this is supposed to be my get-back-up-on-that-horse-and-ride session. It feels like my father is ordering me to go outside to face the neighborhood bully. But, like a good father, Bill is not abandoning me completely. Since my card counting is still less than perfect, I accept Bill's offer to give me the old nudge under the table to raise my bets when the count is high.

It's the middle of a Saturday afternoon, but the tables in the high-limit area are mostly empty.

"This one looks good," Bill says, steering us to a six-deck, $25 minimum table. We're greeted by a middle-aged blond dealer named Helen, who looks like the salt of the earth and sounds like she never spent a day outside the Midwest. I'd expect to find her to be behind the counter at a neighborhood grocery store instead of wearing a checkered vest and dealing blackjack. Right away, Pat and Helen get into a "where are you from?" and "have you ever been to?"

conversation about notable places around the state. Meanwhile, I lay five big ones on the green felt and get my chips.

The pit boss, a tall, thin black man, glides over and asks if I have a players' card. I tell him no, but I'd like to get one. I give him my driver's license and he glides away.

Helen's chitchat dies as she finishes shuffling the cards and she gives me my chips. She starts flipping out two hands to match my bets. I also double the bets on the first hands since Bill tells me the odds are about 50/50. Since no cards have been played the deck is balanced, at least theoretically, in terms of the distribution of high and low cards.

"Usually, you'll win them both or win-one, lose-one," Bill has told me. In this case, I get a blackjack and win the second hand too. I'm off to a blazing start.

Over the next ten minutes, I wait for the nudge under the table, but it never comes. I'm not disappointed since I'm winning just about every hand I play. When I double, she busts. When I split, I win both hands. When she has a 6, her hole card is a 10 and she draws a high enough card to bust. In short, this is exactly the way it's supposed to be. I'm almost chuckling to myself, thinking, "What was I so afraid of?"

Throughout the session, Bill's low, reassuring voice is like an air traffic controller guiding me in for a smooth landing. He sees things I don't and reminds me of things I forget. He is adjusting my basic strategy plays as the count rises and falls, but never quite enough to warrant a higher bet.

"Double that . . ." he says when I get a soft hand, an ace, 7 against the dealer's 6, a hand that frequently confuses me. "Wave them both," he says when I get a 16 and 15 facing a dealer's 10. While I'm hearing his actual voice, it's as if his voice is in my head. And I realize it's been there in all the sessions I've played since I took up this game. It's a bit like the voice of my mother, now gone from this world, but still in my conscience in so many ways. Similarly, Bill firmly reminds me to always do the right thing.

Sometime during this amazing session, the pit boss appears at my side, lays my newly minted players' card at my elbow, and softly and slowly whispers, "California Phil . . ." I laugh as he walks away, a distant corner of my brain wondering what he was implying by nicknaming me.

A short time later—which almost felt like no time at all—I come out of the other end of a tunnel, look down, and see I have an ample stack of green chips. There are chips everywhere, tumbling across the table, spilling across the felt in a happy, jolly mess.

"I think that'll do it for me," I say, trying to be suave but probably sounding more like a young man after the first time he's had sex.

And Helen—dear Helen, who has generously dealt me so many kings and aces, and saved all the bust cards for her hand—leans in closely with her stern, practical, Midwestern face. Apparently my giddy expression alarms her.

"You see that sign over there?" she whispers. "It says, 'Cashier.' You're going to go over there and cash in these chips and then you're going to leave the casino. And you're not going to spend a penny of all this on the way out."

I almost reply, "Yes, Mom." Instead, I nod and smile foolishly.

Helen colors me up, turning my green chips into two purple chips, two black chips, and assorted greens. Looking down into my sweating hand, I realize this is another historic milestone in my blackjack career. This is the first time I've gotten two $500 chips in one session. At the cashier's window I discover the total amount of my win is $760. And if you have been paying attention you will be surprised by the same thing that amazed me: that is nearly the exact total I lost in Des Moines and Joliet. So, as far as my trip goes, I'm up nearly a grand.

Despite all the brave rhetoric Bill and I exchange about the math in blackjack, and the integrity of the statistics and bell curves, there seems to be a greater equalizing force at work in the universe. You can't prove it in a lab, but I feel it at work in my life despite my best efforts to reject all notions of higher powers. It is like a great swinging pendulum, so heavy that no human can change its course or defy its power. And it doles out good days and bad days, good sessions and bad sessions, with unemotional equality and total certainty.

After my joyous trip to the cage, where I receive my winnings and tuck those bills back into my pocket, Bill says, "I think I'll play a little," and we head back to the tables. Helen has been replaced by a dealer named Tom, a square-headed, good-natured Swede with deep-set eyes and an overly loud voice. He converts Bill's $500 into chips and starts dealing.

Bill focuses.

Right away, it looks like trouble. Gone is the cheerful busting Helen, the congratulations she gave me for "good hits" and smart stands. I can't help but feel that Tom is playing *against* Bill. It makes me think how Humble and Cooper, writing in *The World's Greatest Blackjack Book*, said that a survey has shown that players win more from women dealers than from men. Of course, in the old days, a big part of the game was to make sure the dealer wasn't cheating. But players still feel that some dealers are hot, and others are not. Am I reading too much into all this? Or is this another one of those intangibles, along with confidence, that Bill alluded to? After all, Bill's skill is greater than any negative vibe any dealer can throw out. Still, as Pat and I watch, we realize this will be a struggle.

For about ten minutes, Bill is up a little, then down a little. He wins one hand, then loses or pushes the other. It's like a force field of tension that needs to be broken. Yet it's unclear whether, once broken, Bill's fortunes will skyrocket or plummet. Then, slowly, agonizingly, the slide begins when he loses several big bets. His stack of chips is shrinking. Finally, in the middle of a split, he stands up and digs three hundred more from his pocket.

"When money starts flying out of his pockets I usually go for a walk," Pat tells me later. This time, though, she stays to watch.

I've seen it happen too. And I've seen Bill bounce back, recoup all his losses, and walk away a winner. But it isn't happening today. Finally, he stands.

"I'm done," he says, and tosses a chip to the dealer as a tip.

I know better than to ask, but I have noticed that he has lost $800. That's the exact amount he won last night.

And so the pendulum swings first toward fortune and then loss.

"I could have beat that game if I had the time," Bill says as we walk back through the casino.

There's something strange about this whole thing for me. Finally, I realize what it is. I've never seen Bill lose before. He's told me many times about his losses but, like an idolizing sports fan, I thought he was unbeatable. *Say it ain't so, Bill.*

"It's no big deal," Bill says. "I'll get the money back and more next time I'm at the table."

Bill is way better about losing than I am. My system for handling a big loss is very simple: I whine and moan and question my manhood. Bill is more analytical. He has told me that in the early days of his career, after a bad session, he would, "lie awake, staring at the ceiling and replaying the hands, wondering if I did anything wrong." Still, I can see that the loss irks him. There is a heaviness in the car as we drive back to his house.

The difference between Bill and me is that he has fifteen years of playing and has seen nearly every cycle the game has to offer. There is no more staring at the ceiling in the middle of the night. He knows this is part of the game. If you don't have the stomach for it, he often says, find another game. This $800 loss is a drop in the bucket compared to many of his sessions. And when you add it all up, it comes out to this simple formula Bill told me early on: "I win seven out of ten times, and when I win, I win more money than when I lose."

As we pull back into the driveway, Bill seems to have processed the loss. And the heaviness lifts.

"I told Father Andy you were in town," Bill says. "He really enjoyed meeting you in Vegas so I invited him over for dinner. He's coming with a woman from our church."

"It will be great to see him again," I say.

Until they arrive, Bill and I sit outside, have a drink, and relax by—what else?—playing a few hands of blackjack.

Chapter 14

A Divine Bankroll

"Cast in thy lot among us; let us all have one purse."
—Proverbs 1:12-14

Bill tells me that he does his best to keep his blackjack playing a secret, especially from his business associates and members of his Catholic church. The problem, he tells me, is that people just don't understand what he's really doing. When they hear that he counts cards they want to tell him that it doesn't work and you can't possibly win. Others say they heard it was illegal or cheating. And still others just think he is exaggerating his wins and diminishing his losses.

As I work on this book, I notice that my friends have a similar response. I thought a good friend of mine, the chief financial officer for an Internet company, would enjoy hearing about the book. After all, he makes his living with money and numbers. But it becomes clear that his mind is closed. Every time I mention I've been learning to count cards, he says, "I swear, they're going to find you dead in an alley somewhere."

So, over time, I become careful about whom I tell about my blackjack playing.

Still, Bill tells me, the word sometimes gets out. A number of years ago, a new priest, Father Andy, came to Bill's church and they slowly developed a friendship. Eventually, they began meeting every Wednesday morning for coffee. One day, Bill was in the church offices while Father Andy was putting on his clerical collar. They started chatting and discovered they were both going to be in Las Vegas that weekend. They arranged to meet.

It turned out that the priest loved playing video poker. Bill invited him to come sit at the table and watch him play blackjack.

"He seemed pretty impressed," Bill recalls.

So impressed, it turned out, that Father Andy came to Bill with a proposition.

"I've put together a little bankroll," the priest confided. "I'd be honored if you played it for me."

This wasn't the first time Bill had taken money from investors. The MIT team usually played from a $150,000 bankroll from investors. Private investors also come to Bill on a regular basis, wanting him to play with their money and share in his profits. In most cases, Bill turns down these offers since he doesn't really like a business relationship with people he doesn't know very well. But with Father Andy, Bill offered him a 70/30 split on all profits and a 50/50 split on all losses. They went to Las Vegas together. At the end of the trip, Bill handed the priest $2,500, his share of the winnings.

"He was pretty happy about that," Bill says in his understated way.

This arrangement continued with Bill keeping Father Andy informed about lucrative games. When one of Bill's local casinos opened a two-deck game with favorable rules, Bill made the customary offer to the clergyman.

Father Andy replied, "I'm in for a grand. Drop by the rectory. I'll leave an envelope for you."

We are still out in the backyard playing blackjack when Bill tells me these stories. The doorbell rings and a few minutes later I shake hands with Father Andy and his assistant, Karen. It's good to see Father Andy again, and here in this setting, he seems more relaxed than when I saw him in Las Vegas. Still, he retains that quiet, watchful presence. Karen is more outspoken, lively with sudden explosive laughter. They are both relaxed and apparently happy to talk about blackjack, gambling, and their unusual relationship with Bill.

"Remember the priest we met on the Strip?" Father Andy asks, chuckling.

"Oh man," Bill says, wincing. He turns to me. "This guy had the white collar and everything. He was out there on the Strip quoting the Bible and was asking for money for his parish or some school or something. We mentioned him to someone in the hotel we were staying at and it turned out the guy had nothing to do with any church at all. It was all just a con."

"It was sad, really," Father Andy says, without any bitterness. "I often wonder what happened to him."

There is a special quality to the way that Father Andy and Karen answer questions. Their responses are thoughtful, careful, and deeper than what you get from most people. I'm dying to ask one question in particular, but here, it seems a little inappropriate, since Pat has fixed such a nice dinner and this is more of a get-to-know-you than an ask-tough-questions situation. So I get Father Andy's email address and write him sometime later. I get no reply. I write a second time, assuring him I would not use his real name since I assume some of his parishioners wouldn't look kindly on his Vegas trips, even if they pump money into the church.

The next day I get an answer to my email.

"My apologies for not getting back to you more quickly," Father Andy's email begins. "As a rule I don't look at my email over the weekend (for obvious reasons). Fortunately at Mass yesterday Bill mentioned that you had sent me a couple of questions."

I picture the scene in the church following Mass: the echoing sounds in the large space, the organ music, the people chatting in low tones, the shuffling of feet and banging of the kneeling benches. And then I visualize Bill in the scene. I can picture him looking quiet and thoughtful, almost stern. And yet, this is an expression I've seen on his face at the blackjack table, too. I wonder how many of his fellow parishioners would recognize him if they bumped into him in a casino, his face friendly but businesslike, his dark eyes focused on winning.

In my email, I asked Father Andy to describe his relationship with Bill and to give me any insights into his personality that he's gleaned from their time and travels together.

"I would describe my relationship with Bill and Pat as a good friendship," Father Andy writes. "We share similar views in matters of faith and have had some comparable experiences in working for and with the Church We also tend to agree on politics and obviously both enjoy gambling, though I on a much smaller scale than Bill. We meet for breakfast weekly in part because I think Bill is a deeply spiritual man and the primary reason he no longer works in the Church is economic—church salaries are not conducive to supporting a family. Thus I become a conduit, as it were, to what is happening in the day-to-day life of the diocese and parish. On my part, it is helpful to have a supportive voice that is not afraid of challenging me from time to time. As with any friendship between a pastor and a parishioner there are certain boundaries I cannot and do not cross. I never share nor would Bill expect me to share Church information of a confidential nature.

"Bill can be a 'hard read,' which might be partly why he is so successful in card counting. I see him as an intelligent, thoughtful, and reflective person who has a kind and even sensitive heart. Bill is very observant and, I think, reads a person as well as he does cards! He is also strong-willed and highly principled—there are certain lines he will not cross."

This makes me think of our first trip to Las Vegas when the drunken woman came on to Bill as he was heading to the cashier's cage. "I've never cheated on Pat and I never will," he told me. That was clearly one line he would not cross.

"And, I think if others cross this line with Bill," Father Andy's email continues, "my guess is that he might not completely 'write them off' but, and I am speculating here, I would think he might have a strong temper when pushed to that point. In short, Bill has a lot of patience but don't go beyond his limit—or else!"

This is what I thought of as the mobster side of Bill's personality. He exudes a deep, quiet conviction.

"He is something of an enigma. By that I mean I find it intriguing how someone with the ability to concentrate on counting cards and is clearly very intelligent can at the same time not remember the time his plane departs [or] where he left his keys or parked his car. The times we have traveled together I noticed I'm the one who keeps track of all that and Bill is often asking almost as if it is data he just cannot 'get.'"

Next came an answer to the most important question I had wanted to ask at dinner that night at Bill's. However, I left it to ask in this email exchange: Why does he gamble? And, more generally speaking, how does the Church view gambling? Although I, myself, do it, I can't get away from the feeling that there is something wrong with it, something slightly sinful and counter to religious teachings.

"As for gambling, the Catholic view has always been far more tolerant than that of evangelical Christians," he writes. And all I can think as I read this is, *No wonder Catholicism is one of the world's most popular religions.*

"Basically the Church teaches that games of chance are not wrong in and of themselves and are morally acceptable provided one is not gambling with what he or she needs to meet their material obligations. So if one is gambling with the mortgage money, or money that is needed for food or to keep the lights on, then it is immoral. There is also the danger of addiction.

"Personally, I see myself only as a recreational gambler. I could not afford to play at Bill's level and am very comfortable not doing so. You recall that Pat and I walk away when his stakes start getting too high for us. I am fine winning a few hundred dollars (unless I hit a royal flush) and feel more security knowing that is all I might lose as well. The truth is [that] I just enjoy playing video poker. While it relies more on luck than does blackjack, there is enough of a strategy that I have to do a little mental work and have a small part in what the results might be."

As I read his next words I get goose bumps because the thought is so well expressed.

"From the perspective of faith, I have sometimes said that faith itself is a gamble—one is taking a chance on God. It is not an unreasonable chance, but there is no guarantee and of course this holds true (though in reverse) for the non-believer as well. As a priest, I have chosen to stake my career and my life on this 'wager.' Perhaps I am just covering my bet, but over the years I have become convinced in the constant yet minority Christian position that holds to universal salvation. Thus I am firmly convinced that people of faith need to focus their efforts on this life and this world and entrust their ultimate future to God. With that, I'll end my homily!"

As I read Father Andy's words, "one is taking a chance on God," I think how many people can't deal with things that are a matter of faith. They want definite answers and they want them now, not sometime in the hazy future. That is the challenge of faith.

I also see a second meaning to Father Andy's message. Yes, we need faith in the events of our lives. But playing blackjack requires faith, too, since the cards you count predict the future. But as every card counter knows, while there is a higher probability, there are still no guarantees. If we get an 11 against a dealer's 10, we always double because it is a beautiful opportunity for success. But we have to have faith that our hit card will be a 10 for 21. Or that the dealer's hole card will be a 6 for 16, setting up a dealer bust on the third card.

In my own case, I was raised by a mother who prayed every morning and a father who proudly demanded "proof" before he would consider that God existed. And now, here was my new friend, Bill, who always knew the count at a blackjack table, but was still willing to take a chance on God. What did that say about him? Maybe Bill believed that we control those things that are within our power to control—such as the cards in blackjack—and we leave everything else to God.

Pondering these thoughts made me think back to a difficult time I had in my own life some years ago. I had what I thought was going to be my big break: a young and up-and-coming Hollywood producer named Barin Kumar optioned a screenplay I wrote and we began to collaborate on a rewrite of the script. It was going to be his big breakthrough picture and it would introduce me as the next serious screenwriter. If the movie went into production—and he had raised half the budget—I would get about a million dollars. The movie was a thriller about industrial fraud in an airline parts factory.

As we worked together on the script, I often met with Barin at a bar near my house in Long Beach where workers from the Boeing airline manufacturing plant came for a beer after work. On the walls of the bar were pictures of planes and jets made in the factories nearby, signed by the test pilots who flew them. This local lore was the perfect creative backdrop for our brainstorming. On one visit to the bar, Barin found a poem on the wall by a pilot who had been killed in World War II. The last line of the poem describes how, when he was flying, he felt like he could "put out my hand, and touch the face of God."

The rewrite was nearing completion when I flew back to New England for the holidays. On Christmas Eve I got a phone call; Barin had died of a massive heart attack. He was only thirty-six. I was devastated on both a personal and professional level. A few weeks later I returned to our hangout, the bar with all the airline memorabilia, to hold a private memorial service for my friend. I drank a few beers and reread the poem, wondering if Barin had a premonition of his death. I kept searching for an explanation for this tragedy. No answers came to me.

Later, as I drove home, I looked up at the sky and saw that it was filled with sunlit golden clouds and, closer, an enormous flock of seagulls in flight. It struck me how vast and unknowable the universe is. At that moment it came to me that I would never know why Barin had met such an untimely death. Only the mind of God was large enough to see why this had to happen. While it was painful, it was the beginning of a new phase in my life, one in which I stopped looking for absolute answers. Furthermore, you don't always know what is fortune and what is misfortune; today's bad luck can be tomorrow's salvation. At the tables, an early losing hand sets up a later blackjack with more money riding on it. We can't know the results of our actions for many years. Only God understands the tapestry of life being woven each day.

That night in Bill's backyard, we talk about blackjack, gambling, and the excesses of Las Vegas. We talk long into the night. And then the next day I say good-bye to Bill and Pat and head back out on the road. As I drive, though, new thoughts tumble around in my mind about Bill and blackjack. And chance. And faith.

Chapter 15

Casino in the Woods

"Everyone's calling on God or Jesus for something . . . 'Ohhhh God let me have an 8, let me have a 6, let me have a 10 down on that double down. Please if you just . . .' And if you multiply that by all the people playing and begging and all those numbers coming up at the same time and you know God can't figure out who to send what to what so God just says, 'Bust everybody!'"
—Bill Cosby

A **few days later, with** no further car problems, I pull into the Boston area where I was raised and where my father, brother, and sister still live. My brother, Pete, is in a suburb of Boston and my father and sister, Kate, live in a quaint little town in the middle of the state. Several years ago my parents bought a classic New England house, built in 1840, right on the town square. My mother had one happy year here, then got sick, declined quickly, and died. Now, my eighty-six-year-old father says he "rattles around" in the huge house that is "a millstone around my neck." My brother has an interesting theory: he says that Dad is mad at the house because he thinks it killed my mother.

Several months ago, my father began dating a much younger woman he met on the Internet, and it worries my brothers and sister since it seems he might even try to marry her.

As I approach Massachusetts I catch word through the family grapevine that the new girlfriend has temporarily moved in with my dad. I decide to stay at my brother's house instead just to avoid the whole issue. However, my dad calls me and asks, "Are you still into blackjack?"

I tell him I am.

"Let's go to Foxwoods. Wiki says it's the second biggest casino in the world." My dad loves the Internet and frequently interrupts conversations to Google questions on his iPhone. He's a huge Apple computer guy, too, and bought stock in the company, which my father monitors hourly.

I call Bill and ask him if he's played at Foxwoods.

"Many times," he says at once. "We used to hit that place with the MIT team all the time. You can probably find a great two-deck game there." Then he adds, "I really think you have to change your count away from the Knock Out. The Knock Out is okay but the Zen is much stronger." Apparently he's been ruminating on this since I left his house.

"Did you use that count with the teams?"

"No, actually, we used the Hi-Lo," he says. "It was easier to teach and then we were all on the same page. The Hi-Lo is really the gold standard for team play."

Again, I can't help imagining what it would be like to be in Bill's head. He uses the Zen or the Hi-Lo. Then he hits the switch in his head again and sees what the Knock Out is showing. He compares his bets and can see which wins more money. Meanwhile, I still have shaky hands and a cloudy grasp of any advantage I might have over the house.

"Sorry to keep harping on this count," Bill says. "I just don't want any of my students to be half-assed."

I don't say so, but I'm proud that he takes such a personal interest in my success. I flash back on his early prediction: "You're going to make so much money." And, in fact, I have nearly $1,000 in my bankroll to prove it. But I want more. And, more than the money, I want to master the count so I can feel confident at the table.

A few days later I meet my father in the parking lot of a Dunkin' Donuts near his house. He's driving his red 2010 Volkswagen Sport-Wagen TDI, which he bought because he thinks it makes him look younger. And he does look amazingly young. He's got a snow-white fringe of hair around his tanned, bald head. His eyes twinkle and he walks easily with his hands folded behind his back—the pose of a professor deep in thought. He's charming and alert and everyone loves him. When I travel with him, people smile at me as if to say, "Aw, look, he's taking care of his father." Once, in Oakland, California, a middle-aged black woman saw us together and grabbed my arm. "Keep your father close to you," she implored. "He needs you."

I drive the rest of the way to Foxwoods talking up a storm with my father. As we turn off the interstate, I think how strange it is to find the world's second largest casino out here in the middle of the woods. After we park and walk into the lavish entryway, with a humongous chandelier hanging overhead, I can feel my father's spirits rise. He loves casinos; probably because of the lights, the color, the music, and the excitement in the air. He's not at all worried that I might become addicted to gambling or lose too much money. He seems to immediately grasp the concept of the bell curve and the math that shows I'll be an eventual winner. It's funny because he's actually more optimistic than I am.

Foxwoods is an incredible spectacle and so different than the Vegas casinos. It is really more like a giant shopping mall connecting a string of casinos decorated in Native American art. One long escalator runs next to a glass wall looking out over a canopy of dense forest spreading out in all directions.

We scout out all the various casinos but there are no two-deck games on the floor, only in the high-limit areas. The high-limit areas are still intimidating to me so I look for a $10 game I can play out on the floor. I'm nervous but excited and want to practice counting. It seems that I do a little too much scouting, though, as I look behind and notice that my dad is really dragging. So I see two open seats at a nearby six-deck game and decide to sit down. I'm at third base and an attractive young blonde sits to my immediate right, smoking a cigarette. The smoke is like a needle in my eye. As she bets wildly, and loses, she pulls $100 bills from the depth of her generous cleavage.

I nudge my dad and nod toward the blonde: "Dad, check it out."
He catches an eyeful and smiles at me.

I buy in for two hundred and get a healthy stack of $5 chips. It feels pretty low-key playing for small stakes in such a diluted deck. As Bill has told me, in a six-deck game the count rises and falls gradually. That's why blackjack teams play six-deck games: the count gets high and stays there, giving the Big Player a chance to sit down and play six hands on a high count. In two-deck games it's more volatile and can be super high one hand and back to neutral the next. In one-deck games you're always only a few cards away from a high count, and a reshuffle. That's probably why I did well in Wendover, because I didn't have to keep the count for very long.

Today, I start with a count of negative 20 since I'm still using what Bill implied was the "half-assed" Knock Out count. In the first shoe I lose about $100 and the count never gets higher than 3 or 4. That means I go from my basic bet of $10 (I couldn't stand betting just $5, even though it's allowed) to $20 or $30. In the second shoe I begin to get a clearer picture of the count despite the dual distraction of the smoke in one eye and my good eye being drawn to the cleavage of my playing partner as she whips out a steady stream of hundreds from the deep crevasse. An old woman, apparently her mother, materializes by the table, asking how she is doing, and I'm suddenly treated to a sobering picture of what this hot young blonde will look like in a few decades. It's enough to make me refocus my attention on the cards. Even my dad stops ogling her.

As I settle down and grow more confident about the count, I increase my bets and win several splits and doubles. My dad is following the action and seems impressed, especially since the other players at the table keep buying in for more chips. But then the sad truth hits me: I'm really not going to win much here, betting like this. But maybe I can win enough to buy us a nice seafood lunch. A few hands later I cash out, a $50 winner, and leave the smoker and her mom behind us. At the cage, I get my winnings and also a hot tip on a good restaurant about twenty miles south on the water.

We go to a seafood restaurant on the water called Abbott's. And, nearby is—you guessed it—another restaurant called Costello's. My dad wanders off as I photograph the Lexus to prove to readers of our blogs that this old car made it all the way to the East Coast. As I walk back to find my dad, I see he is sitting on the steps of the restaurant deck, his head cocked, reading something on his iPhone. There is something vulnerable and even childlike about his pose. I still have my camera out and take a picture of him. A few weeks later, that picture, freezing him in that pose, becomes very important to me.

Soon, it's time for me to leave New England and head back to California. I have a nice dinner with my sister and my dad and afterward we go out for ice cream at a farm stand. As we drive around, enjoying the beautiful New England spring evening, with mist rising from the fields, my father says, "Phil, it's so nice to have you here." It's not like him to say this kind of thing. And when he repeats it several times, I get a sense of foreboding and a chill runs through me.

My next stop is Cleveland, and before I get there I have a story to tell about my best friend from childhood. His name was Steve and we were very close friends until after graduation from college, when he went to Europe. There, he met and married a French woman and settled in a small village north of Marseilles. They had three sons, one named Bernard, who became my godson. Steve worked various sales jobs, traveling around Europe to support his family. But judging from the tone of his letters, I sensed that Steve was leading a life that he hated.

One day, I got a call from his parents saying that Steve had disappeared. The police found his car abandoned at Orly Airport in Paris with no note explaining where he had gone. His parents called me hoping that Steve had come to visit me. But he hadn't and I didn't hear from him either.

That was twenty-five years ago. Since then, I've often wondered if Steve is still alive. I wondered if he committed suicide or was maybe living on the streets. I even thought he might have gotten remarried and started a new family. Most of all, I wondered if I'd ever see him again.

Last Christmas, my godson Bernard told me he wanted to find his father. Over the years, I had done some research on my own. At one point, a private investigator I knew gave me an address in Cleveland for Steve but, since he has a common last name, couldn't confirm it was really him. I gave this address to Bernard. He hired someone to pretend he was lost while delivering a pizza and the man who answered the door matched the description of his father. Last winter Bernard took an overnight bus to Cleveland, from his home in New York, and on Christmas Eve knocked on the door. Steve opened the door and immediately recognized his son. "I knew you would come someday!" Steve said. They hugged and cried and talked for several days straight.

Now it was my turn to be reunited with my oldest friend. I had spoken with him on the phone and exchanged emails. He even told me that there was a new casino opening up in Cleveland that we could visit when I came.

I drive all day long from Massachusetts to Cleveland, about seven hundred miles. Along the way, I catch a bug of some kind and begin to feel real crappy. But I can't stop driving—I have to make it to Steve's. So I pull over every two hours and sleep in rest areas. Finally, at about 9 p.m., and thoroughly exhausted, I knock on the door, and it's opened by my oldest friend.

"You look just the same!" Steve exclaims, shaking my hand warmly.

I wish I could say the same for Steve. When I last saw him he was tall, slim, and youthful. Now he must weigh nearly three hundred pounds and some of his teeth are missing. But, after this initial shock, I see that in all other ways, he looks healthy and, yes, even unchanged. He has a full head of blond hair, with a touch of silver appearing, and he has a ruddy, energetic look. His modest house, in a working-class Cleveland neighborhood, is filled with books and echoes with classical music.

Over wine and a good meal (which I hardly touch in my sickened state) I tell him I'm playing blackjack from coast to coast. I jokingly invite him to come along. He shocks me when he takes me up on the offer, deciding to ride along as far as Denver and then fly back.

We make a brief stop at the new Horseshoe Casino in Cleveland, which is in a stately old granite building right in downtown. It's a Friday morning but it may as well be New Year's Eve in the casino. Every seat is taken. I feel a little self-conscious revealing my new vice to my old friend, but Steve enjoys the spectacle of it all. I just can't find a table to play at, though, so we hit the road and continue west.

As the old Lexus cruises past miles of cornfields, we grow more comfortable and, finally, I ask him the big question: Why did he leave his wife and three sons?

"I was nuts," he says, matter-of-factly. "I was crazy, probably manic depressive, and suicidal. I had to get away or—or I didn't know what I would do." He adds that his wife was increasingly cruel to him.

"Before I left on my sales calls, she'd say, 'If you don't sell enough, don't bother coming home.' Eventually, I didn't."

After living in Washington, DC, for a short time, Steve wandered to Danville, Indiana, the little town where we had both lived when we were in first grade. Still deeply depressed, Steve lived in a shabby motel on the outskirts of that town and worked in a paint factory near Indianapolis, even though, years earlier, he had earned an MBA from the University of California, Berkeley. Thoughts of suicide stalked him constantly.

"But what saved me," Steve said, "was something I read in a book at your house once when I was visiting. It said a high percentage of people who commit suicide have had a suicide in their immediate family. I knew of no suicides in my family so I began to hope I would be able to resist the urge to kill myself."

Eventually, Steve rebuilt himself psychologically, largely by working a string of menial jobs that proved he could work with his hands and take care of himself.

"There was something about solving problems in the real world, with my hands, that got me out of my head and gave me the self-confidence I needed." Now, Steve works a union job in a factory in Cleveland, rebuilding alternators for locomotives. He has his own work station where he labors for up to twelve hours a day, bathed in sweat. Then he showers, returns home, and reads *The Odyssey* in Greek.

That spring afternoon, Steve and I make a Capra-esque visit to our old homes in Danville, Indiana, the same town where we lived when we were both six years old. We find the houses we used to live in, see our old school, and have lunch in a diner on the town square. Then we push on across the Midwest until a violent thunderstorm drives us to seek shelter in a motel in Missouri. The next morning, Father's Day, we drive on in beautiful, sunny weather.

I carry with me a list of casinos along my route and I tell Steve I need to play at the Isle of Capri in Boonsville. It's a small casino located near the center of this picturesque little Midwestern town. It blends in with the other buildings, pretending to be as wholesome as the local Chevy dealership. In the parking lot Steve says he's not going in with me. Instead, he hangs his binoculars around his neck and produces a field guide of local birds. He tells me he'll go for a walk while I play blackjack. We stand there, weighing the irony of the moment.

"You're going bird-watching and I'm going to play blackjack," I say. "I guess we've gone in different directions."

"Yes," he says, smiling. "But after all these years, we're still good friends."

He turns and ambles away, keeping his ear cocked for birdcalls.

Inside the casino, all that's available is a six-deck game where a tall, white-haired man sits behind a stack of green chips. As I settle into the game, the middle-aged dealer stretches her back and grimaces painfully.

"If you need a prescription," my playing partner says, "I've got my pad in the truck."

She laughs, gives him a hit card, and he busts.

"You're a doctor?" I ask.

"Most of the time I am," he answers. "But today, I'm a drinker and a gambler."

Another guy joins us and runs through his stack of chips in a flurry of losing hands. He vanishes, then reappears and buys back in with several hundred dollars. Moments later, his wife appears and surveys his chip pile.

"You're doing pretty well," she observes.

"No," he says sadly. "I just went to the ATM."

Meanwhile, I'm not doing so well either. I'm down at least one hundred.

Yet another guy joins us. We could be a foursome waiting to tee off at the local municipal golf course instead of four gamblers indoors on a sunny Sunday morning. I don't know why but, in a rare burst of extraversion, I look around the table and call out: "Gentlemen, I just want to say one thing to you all: Happy Father's Day!"

"Yay!" They all cheer and toast with their beers and I with my coffee.

Moments later, the count shoots up and I raise my bets. And then—I kid you not—I get four blackjacks in a row. I think of it as my Father's Day present. This bonanza not only brings me back but I win another $50. It's not much, but it beats the hell out of losing and will pay for a few meals along the road.

After a long, hot drive across Kansas and half of Colorado, I pull into the Denver airport and step out with Steve. As we shake hands, I realize there is so much more to say. But it will have to wait for the next time we meet. It's just great to know that now, we are back in touch, and that there will be a next time.

I push on, stopping for the night with my younger brother, Kevin, and his family in the mountains above Denver. I consider playing the casinos in Central City. But time is passing and I need to get back home. Besides, it's a stunning day for a drive through the Rockies, and I don't want to spend it indoors, surrounded by cigarette smokers. I enjoy the drive through the soaring Front Range, and then the long haul across Utah's canyon country. Finally, I stop an hour north of Nevada in Cedar City, Utah. I check in, eat dinner, and practice my card counting.

I head out early the next morning. The first town over the line is Mesquite, which once had four casinos. One is vacant now, weeds pushing up through the parking lot asphalt and flies beating against the insides of the windows. It's a lonely, spooky sight. I thought the house always wins. But here, nature is taking over again.

I find two casinos across the street from each other. I decide to use the hit-and-run strategy that brought me success in Wendover. There's an open two-deck game with a $10 table limit. I win $175 in about fifteen minutes and walk across the street to the other casino. There, I find a bunch of locals in a six-deck game betting $5 a hand. They are what casino managers refer to as "grazers," playing for hours without winning or losing much. I play for nearly a half hour, winning probably $100. Then, nearby, a two-deck opens up. I scoop up my chips and I move over. The dealer is a young Hispanic guy who tells me he has two kids to support so he never gambles. He deals at a nice, steady pace, paying little attention to my betting, and I find that I'm able to keep the count. After several shoes I go on a hot streak, winning several doubles and a split. I know I'm up, but don't know how much. When someone else sits down, I cash out and find I've won $250 and $425 for the day.

I'm tempted to try the third casino in town, but I also don't want to erase my wins. So I call an end to my cross-country trip and, as I drive off, I take a final tally. Thanks mainly to my big win in Wendover, I've made $1,400 for the trip. It's not a fortune but, unlike most other travelers who return from vacation broke, I actually made money.

The strangest part is driving through Las Vegas and not stopping. But as I look at the towering casinos, so improbable and stark in the desert sun, I know I'll be here in another month. Bill and I are already planning our next blackjack adventure.

Chapter 16

Standard Deviation Revisited

"Just relax and have a good time!"
—Blackjack dealer while beating a player out of $2,000

After my wins at blackjack tables across the country, my confidence is high as I drive to Las Vegas on a Sunday afternoon, about a month after returning from my coast-to-coast trip. I feel my card counting still needs work, but I've made real progress. The only thing holding me back is the stakes I play for. I know I'll never make money unless I play for $25 or $50 a hand instead of the $5 and $10 tables I played at on my trip. The problem is, the high stakes make me too nervous. And when I get nervous I can't keep the count as well. So, on this trip I decide to try to push myself out of my comfort zone because, well, I'm ready to make some real money.

Or, at least I think I am.

I'm passing Baker, California—where the world's tallest thermometer (at least according to their website) rises toward the desert sky—when my phone rings. It's Bill, who flew in earlier and has already been at the tables on the Strip.

"I've played two sessions and I'm already down $1,600," he says. "But that's okay. I'll win it all back and more."

A chill passes through me. It's been a while since I'd had a big loss but I remember, all too well, what it feels like. And when Bill loses it's twice as bad because I know he's not making the mistakes I make.

Bill has told me many times that mistakes are costly. "All it takes is two mistakes an hour and you've given up your advantage," he says.

This is really bad news for me because I know I do make mistakes. Using the Knock Out, I've improved, and my basic strategy is almost perfect. My only problem is remembering the "soft doubles"—those that include aces. They seem especially hard for my brain to process. I review my flashcards for soft doubles over and over as I drive, but they just don't seem to sink in.

After I check in at the Flamingo, I call Bill and he says he'll come down to my room. I hear a knock on the door and swing it open. Bill fills the doorframe. I'm struck again by his easy posture, his broad smile, his warm handshake, and his soft voice with its subtle, firm edge. I get the sense that being in Las Vegas agrees with him in a way I don't completely understand.

We head over to the Mandalay Bay and settle in at a two-deck game for my first session. Bill offers to keep the count and let me know when the deck is hot. He'll nudge me under the table once, twice, or three times to spread my bets. I agree since, now that the nervousness has started, I lose confidence that I can keep the count.

The link between fear and memory loss is supported by Danielle C. Lapp in her appropriately titled book *Don't Forget!* In the first chapter, "Clearing the Way to Concentration," she writes: "You can expect memory lapses when your emotions take over and when the situation does not allow you to sustain attention."

Boy, that's a perfect description of being at the blackjack table. When I think back on different blackjack sessions I've played, and recall how I felt, it's as if I was looking at the cards through the wrong end of a telescope. Counting the cards requires so much focus, I can't see anything else. In her book, Lapp provides a list of factors that limit memory: rushing, and being anxious, interrupted, and distracted. All of this perfectly describes my feelings at the blackjack table. So I realize my challenge is to deal with these factors and try to become comfortable while counting cards.

Of course, comfort comes with experience. Still, I try to identify the factors that make me comfortable so I can seek them out at casinos. The dealer is a big part of the comfort factor. I like dealers who at least *pretend* to be on my side. This can even just be a sympathetic wince, as the dealer lays a 5 on her 16 to make 21 and beats my two face cards. More importantly, I like dealers who deal the cards slowly and deliberately. Some dealers even pause respectfully before they gather up your chips after they win.

Over the course of this year, I keep notes on where I play and how much I win. A pattern begins to emerge and I see I often win at some casinos and usually lose at others. Eventually, I create a checklist of elements that seem to contribute to winning sessions beyond just the rules of the specific game, such as standing on soft 17 or doubling after split. Here is what I've noted:

- Is the dealer male or female? I seem to feel more comfortable with women dealers and ultimately win more. Male dealers often try to compete with the player and show who's boss.
- What is the table limit? At this point, $25 a hand works well for me. Playing for more than that, with my restricted bankroll,

is too stressful. So if I play two hands of $25 against the dealer, and spread to $150, I can make a lot of money in a hurry.

- Is the dealer fast or slow? I like slower, deliberate dealers. If I get a fast dealer, I try to set a different pace. But all too often, I try to match their faster speed rather than force them to play slower.

- Is the dealer talkative? This is important for me because I'm naturally curious about people and want to chat. But when I'm playing blackjack, there's a lot at stake so I need to keep my mouth shut and concentrate. I small-talk in between shoes while the dealer is shuffling but then I concentrate while playing.

- Where is the table located in the casino? Like a table in a restaurant, I want to feel comfortable. I like tables on the back-side of a pit without a lot of foot traffic behind me. It's also nice to play in attractively lit casinos like the Wynn rather than depressing dungeons or cramped, noisy casinos like the Nugget or the D.

- Can I play two hands for a single unit? This provides maximum flexibility to raise and lower my bets. If I jump back and forth between one and two hands, it attracts attention from the Eye in the Sky.

- Is there heat? A hovering, suspicious pit boss is a real distraction. A friendly pit boss sets a nice atmosphere.

One thing I've noticed is that the nicer casinos, such as the Wynn, Encore, Bellagio, and Aria, are less crowded and the dealers, pit bosses, and floormen are all polite and seem relaxed. The problem is, the table limits are too high for me—usually $50 or $100 a hand—and that makes me really nervous.

Settling down on the stool at Mandalay Bay, I buy in for $500 and try to play two hands of $25 against the dealer.

"You're gonna need to put $50 on each hand," the dealer snaps.

In other casinos, if you play two hands against the dealer (which is a slight advantage) some casinos require you to double your bet. If you're at the $10 tables, it really doesn't make that much difference. But here, it could be the difference between being wiped out and hanging in there until I catch a good run of cards.

Bill is immediately alert and ready to defend me.

"When did that happen?" he asks.

"It's always been like that," says a pit boss who has overheard our conversation.

"I've been here before and that wasn't required," Bill states. "Could you check on that for us?"

I admire Bill's ability to be persistent and polite at the same time.

Meanwhile, I've got $100 across two hands and my confidence evaporates before I even begin. I lose the first hand. And then I lose most of the rest of the shoe. Eventually, I run out of chips and buy in for another $200. I lose that too and I'm done and out of there in about twenty minutes to the tune of a $700 loss. I never had a chance to get comfortable and Bill never signaled that I had a positive count.

But since Bill's losses have already surpassed mine, I don't complain.

As we walk out of the casino, Bill asks, "Did you keep the count?"

"Not really."

Bill is quiet for a moment, then says, "It's been over six months now."

I know all too well what he means.

"When I get shelled like that I have trouble counting."

"You're going to have to learn."

Anger bubbles up. I just took a big loss and now I get a scolding. I think of a lot of things I could say but somehow, I keep my mouth shut.

We move on to the Mirage. Bill says the guys on the MIT team called the Mirage the "counters' trap" because it offers a great game but the surveillance guys have a hawk eye for card counters.

This time I lose $400. I haven't even been in Las Vegas for two hours and I'm down $1,100. Still, I don't feel as bad as I did on my first trip here with Bill. I remember feeling that those losses were the end of the world. Now, I see it as a temporary variation that will change soon, but not soon enough.

Over the next day we both lose and lose. And then we lose some more. One of the only bright spots is when Bill decides to play the $100 tables at the Wynn. I'm scared just sitting next to him and see-ing the small stack of $100 chips and realizing how close he is to extinction. In fact, the dealer starts to bleed him pretty quickly. He's down to his last two chips when the pit boss wanders by.

"Can we get a couple of comps for the buffet?" Bill says. "I mean, look, I'm gettin' killed here."

The pit boss's eyes flash toward the few remaining chips on the betting circles.

"Sure, I can arrange that for you," the pit boss says. He goes to one of the computers and begins filling out the comp form. I look back at the table and see that Bill has escaped death. By the time our comps arrive, Bill has won back all his money and cashes out. Net win: two comps to the best buffet ever. And it would have cost us over $100 if we paid.

As we leave the Wynn I glance at my iPhone and see that my sister has texted me. Oh man, I think, this can't be good.

"Dad has been taken to the hospital," she writes. "He fainted at the top of the basement stairs and hit his head. He's in the trauma center. He is stable but he has three broken ribs, punctured lung, bleeding in his head. But he is talking."

I stand there in the doorway of the busy casino, people chattering happily around me, and picture my poor father lying alone on the cold cellar floor.

The drama unfolds in phone calls and text messages as I move from one casino to the next. It turns out that my father broke up with his girlfriend and then went out for a drink. He came home and parked in the back of the house and entered through the basement and walked up a long, narrow flight of stairs. He had bags of groceries in his hands and was fumbling with the door handle when he blacked out and fell backward down a long flight of stairs. He lay at the bottom of the stairs for two hours, covered in groceries, until the tenant, who was renting a room in his house, heard him moaning, found him, and called my sister.

While juggling these phone calls, Bill and I keep playing and losing. We just can't seem to catch a break.

I meet Bill for breakfast and fill him in on all the latest developments with my father. He listens patiently, nodding sympathetically. His own father is about the same age and he understands what I'm going through.

"Sometimes it seems like life gets out of balance," I say. "Everything goes wrong at the same time. I mean, on top of all things I've got this—"

I have to stop. It's just too embarrassing.

"What?" he asks, waiting for me to finish the sentence.

I decide our relationship has progressed to a point where I can share even this indignity.

"Well, I've got this huge festering zit on the end of my nose that's been staring you in the face for the past three days!"

Bill nods. "Yeah, I kind of noticed that," he answers with supreme diplomacy.

We decide to try a new casino, the D, so named because the owners are from Detroit. A wall of pounding music hits us as we walk through the door. Above the bar is a string of big-screen TVs showing football games. In the pit, we find a $25 two-deck table dealt by a young, sandy-haired man who tells us he's from Bulgaria. After the shuffle and cut, he inserts the plastic yellow card about fifteen cards from the end of the two decks.

Bill and I exchange an amazed glance: *deep penetration!* I've never seen a casino put the cut card so close to the end of the deck. This greatly increases our chances, especially toward the end of the shoe.

It's Bill's turn to play and, despite being what he later describes as a "really juicy game," he begins losing. Soon, our dealer is replaced by a young woman with gaping cleavage and little idea of how to shuffle or deal. Since there is no place for a name tag on her skimpy dress, she wears a choker that reads, "Sarah." She gets a lesson in shuffling from the pit boss while I try to keep my eyes away from her bouncing breasts.

It seems like we should be able to kill this game. But Bill plays, and continues to lose and buy in with more money. Soon, the pit boss notices his action and comes over to chat with us. Because of the money Bill is betting the pit boss is slobbering all over him. I guess the D doesn't see many high rollers.

"Anything you need, you got it," the pit boss says several times.

What we really need is a winning hand. The string of bad cards is unbelievable. Every dealer's up card is a 10 or an ace. Every hand for Bill is a 12, 13, or 14, so he has to hit it. When Bill gets two 10s, the dealer puts together a 21 out of nowhere. I keep thinking the cards have to turn. But they don't.

Our dealer, Sarah, leaves our table and climbs up onto a small platform nearby. She starts dancing half-heartedly. I can't help but feel sorry for her. I look around and see another dealer/dancer on another platform and, man, she's really workin' it. I'm lost in this spectacle of quivering flesh when I feel Bill nudge me.

"Look who we're getting next," he says.

I turn and see a six-foot-tall sex goddess approaching our table. She has cannonball breasts that have never known gravity—as if she was drawn by a sex-crazed teenaged cartoonist. It's sad that she felt the need to turn herself into an anatomical freak because in every other way she really is a beautiful woman.

But the cards she deals are not beautiful. Despite her ineptitude as a dealer, the cards are enough to wipe us out. After a few rounds Bill nods toward the pit, where a huddle of suits is conspicuously uninterested in us.

"They're watching us," Bill says. "If you look away, then look back, you'll catch them."

I try it and, sure enough, catch them eyeballing us. It's a shock because, a short time ago, they were kissing Bill's ass, telling him, "Anything you want—you got it."

I watch as a pit boss gets a phone call.

"It's probably a call from upstairs," Bill says as he hits 16 and busts. "I'm about to get backed off."

Bill keeps playing even though he's down about $1,100. Seconds later I feel a presence behind me and turn to see a tall woman in a business suit next to our table. Her face is a mask of official indignation.

"Stop the game," she says to the dealer. "This game is frozen."

People look around, wondering what's happening. The pit bosses assemble. The sycophantic pit boss appears next to the table, providing backup to his boss. Bill quickly sweeps up his remaining chips and pockets them.

"I'm the casino manager," the woman says to Bill. "You cannot play blackjack here anymore."

"But I just lost $1,100," Bill says, laughing in disbelief.

"You are free to play any other game here. But you cannot play blackjack."

"What a joke," Bill says. "I lose money and you're kicking me out. Okay. Whatever."

We slide off our chairs and head for the cage.

"What a bunch of bullshit," Bill says. "That's a hell of a way to do business."

Our losses continue. And so do the texts from my sister telling me about my father's injuries and his treatment. It's touch and go for a while but eventually my father's condition stabilizes. Outside the D, while we're waiting for the valet to bring my car, I feel rotten. As always, Bill reads my thoughts. He stands directly in front of me, as if to get the attention of a shell-shocked soldier.

"Okay now, look. This is exactly where most counters give up. They decide it doesn't work and they just quit and walk away."

Is it a challenge? I certainly don't want Bill to think I'm a quitter. But I want the pain to stop.

"Losing is part of the process," he adds.

"I know that," I answer, trying to keep the annoyance out of my voice. "But this is too much. Have you ever had a losing streak like this?"

"Oh sure. And worse. Sometimes, the whole team played all weekend and lost. But the next week we won. It's just math. You can't keep losing forever."

I'm angry and sulky and depressed. I'm behaving so badly I'm afraid Bill will give up on me. And to make matters worse, this throbbing zit on my nose just gets bigger, as if it has collected all the bad shit in my life and pasted it right on my face. In my despair I wonder if the pimple is actually cancer. That's the kind of thought you get when things are going wrong.

The next morning we have an hour to kill before I drop Bill at the airport.

"You want to hit Mandalay Bay again?" he asks. "Lots of times, when you're heading to the airport, you have a great session and win your money back."

But I can't see that happening. I've lost faith—at least for now—that it will ever be right again. I drop him at the airport and, trying to repair some of the damage I've done, I give him a hug.

For a little variation, I decide to drive home through Laughlin, about ninety miles south of Las Vegas, and scout the casinos there. As I descend the long grade into Laughlin, located on the Colorado River, I see the familiar sight of tall casino towers rising from the desert floor. It's as if the designers know they are attracting a clientele that just doesn't give a damn about aesthetics. Gamblers are so crazed for a fix they lock in on the casino towers like a homing beacon.

When I step out of the car the heat is suffocating—even hotter than Las Vegas. Inside the casino it's a madhouse of senior citizens. It's like they all just got out of some kind of an old folks' school and they're heading for recess. There's hardly room in the aisles to walk. As I watch, another busload of oldsters pulls up and they unload, a-whoopin' and a-hollerin'. Every blackjack table is jammed.

I seek relief in another nearby casino where, miraculously, I find an open two-deck game. The cards are fanned out in front of the dealer in an arc. The dealer spreads her hands invitingly across the felt.

"Want to try your luck?" She purrs seductively.

Then, something happens that amazes and horrifies me. You would think that, after getting pounded for three straight days in Las Vegas, and losing about two grand, I would be ready to murder the first dealer I see. Instead, I notice my hand is in my pocket, fingering the wad of hundreds I still have left. I see myself pulling them out and buying in for $500. It is then that I realize it's in my blood. I want to hear the snap of the cards on the felt and the soft rattle of the chips as they stack up in front of me. I want to see a flood of small cards come out and feel anticipation build as the count rises. I want to see a 10 land on my double down. I want the chance to get blackjack on both hands—*boom, boom*, as Bill would say.

My hand is coming up out of my pocket. But it holds no buy-in money. That's because I hear Bill's voice in my ear asking a question I don't want to answer.

"Did you keep the count?" I hear him ask.

And I hear my own reply: "Not really."

"It's been six months," he says, leaving the implication stark and irrefutable. Even though Bill would never say this, what he means is: "I've taught others players to count much faster. What's wrong with you?"

And I go one step further and articulate what his words imply: "Come on, Phil. Are you slow or something?"

My mind travels back to that eighth grade math class again with Miss Reid waiting for me to answer a problem she knows is beyond my mental ability. I feel the shame all over again. But, now that I'm older, I also feel the determination. I can learn to do this, to count cards, to consistently beat the casinos. In my stubbornness and pride I believe I can win. But I need more time. I need to come back another day to tap the riches of the kingdom.

I return to the present and look into the dealer's eyes.

"What do you say? Want to try your luck?" she repeats, making her gesture toward the cards. She's like a bartender with a bottle ready to pour a drink for an alcoholic. But I need time—and a lot more practice—before I try again.

"Not today, thanks," I say, before turning toward the door . . .

Part Three:
Take the Money

Chapter 17

Blackjack Brain

"Talented people succeed largely because they devote consid-
erable time, attention, and effort to their topic of predilection.
Through training, they develop well-tuned algorithms and clever
shortcuts that any of us could learn if we tried, and that are
carefully devised to take advantage of our brain's assets and get
around its limits."

—Psychologist and neuroscientist Stanislas Dehaene, *The Number Sense*

Shortly after the New Year, 2013, about ten months
after I began playing blackjack, Bill calls and asks me what
my blackjack goal is for the coming year. I'm a big believer
in setting goals so I'd been thinking about my blackjack
goals before he even asks. But, I haven't reached a conclusion yet.
Since I don't have a ready answer, I throw it back on him.

"What's *your* goal for this year?"

"Six figures," he says.

No qualifications or caveats. Just, "Six figures." That's classic Bill.

"Nice," I say. "What do you think would be a realistic goal for me?"

"I'm thinking we should take one trip a month and play out of a common bankroll," he says. "If we do that, and hit 'em hard, you could make $20K."

Okay, $20K. I like the sound of that. That would be a nice addition to my salary. I could buy some extra things for myself or maybe sock it away toward retirement and charities. Or maybe I could finally take flying lessons. With two sons in college, that was never an option. But this additional money would finally get me into the air. Then, I could fly myself to different casinos around the West: Reno, Las Vegas, Laughlin, or Wendover. It's a wonderful dream. Or is it?

"Honestly," I say to him, "if I make even $10K this year playing blackjack I'd be overjoyed."

"You can do that," Bill says quickly. "So here's the lineup: We'll shoot down to Biloxi in February, then hit Tunica in the spring. After that, we can maybe try Foxwoods or the Indian casinos in California. Then do the circuit again."

As often happens when I'm listening to Bill, I feel the excitement building. He's always pushing me out of my comfort zone, beyond what I think are my limits. It's scary. But if I can break through, I'll be in a rare class of players, the smart guys who *take* money from the casinos. Bill has told me that there are probably only 125 professional blackjack players in the world. I could join that group. And it would show I can perform under pressure, despite the well-oiled casino system with its smiley-face exterior masking a black-hearted, corporate soul.

I don't tell Bill but I know these next three trips will either make or break my card-counting experiment. I can feel my wife's patience growing thin. And frankly, it hasn't quite been the money-making venture

I'd imagined. Furthermore, my own tolerance for gutwrenching losses is growing thin. So I decide to give it three more big trips to pan out.

"I was thinking about something else," Bill says, snapping me back to the present.

"What's that?"

"We talked about using a more sophisticated count, like the Hi-Opt 1. But it might be a good idea if you stuck with the Knock Out."

I'm stunned. The Knock Out? Really? He's the one who described it as "half-assed." Does this mean he doesn't think I can handle the more powerful counts with deck estimation, ace side counts, and index numbers?

I ponder this in silence. He senses my reaction.

"You had some nice wins with the Hi-Opt 1. But if you keep the Knock Out count more accurately, you'll actually come out ahead. When you get really solid with it, you can add in the top index plays. Plus, with a simpler count you won't stare at the cards and you can keep up a conversation with the dealer and the pit boss. When you start winning big, you're going to need a good cover."

Bill has, apparently, realized my terrible secret. I still don't have the count down cold. Sure, I've been able to win some money with basic strategy. And sometimes, my big bets are out there when the count is high. But I'm painfully aware that, when I get splits and doubles, I'm so caught up in the outcome of the hand that I lose the count. And the times I tried using the Hi-Opt 1, with the ace side count, created new challenges for me when I actually needed fewer mental tasks.

"I've got another suggestion," he says.

"Okay."

"For this entire year, we only play two-deck games."

"Why?"

"With a six-deck game, if you lose the count, it's a long time until the reshuffle. With the two-deck games, if you lose the count, you can just use basic strategy until you can start the count again."

I know why Bill has made these suggestions: my skills as a counter are lacking. He's seen it. And I've known it. I've been practicing and playing for about nine months and I'm still not rock solid on the count. I try to keep the disappointment out of my voice.

"Let me think this over, Bill."

"Sure. Meanwhile, what week looks good for Biloxi?"

We set a date to meet at the casinos along the Gulf Coast and I hang up. I sit there for a long time, deflated.

Later that day I break out my cards and chips. I begin dealing hands and using the Knock Out system, feeling my brain making the switch back to a different count. I try picturing myself in a casino, trying to look casual and play quickly and smoothly, talking with the dealer as I play.

But it's just not happening.

Then I recall something that I read and that Bill mentioned to me several times.

"If you don't like dealing with negative numbers, reset the starting count," he once said to me.

Normally, the Knock Out starts at negative 4 and I raise my bets at plus 1. But if I started the count at plus 5 I can raise my bet at plus 10, an easier number to remember. This way, I'll rarely have to use negative numbers.

I begin practicing this way, and notice a difference. But still, my brain feels creaky, slow, even while practicing at home. How would I do in a casino? I redouble my practicing. For the next few days I devote myself to counting down decks of cards and timing myself, trying to get below thirty seconds. The best I can manage is thirty-five seconds and sometimes my count is off.

I'm getting really discouraged. Is it just me? Is my brain just too old for this?

Thinking back, I remember the magazine article I read on the plane in Argentina. It strikes me that I need help from an expert. I need to better understand how the brain works and better understand what kind of a brain—besides old—I have. I begin sending requests to different university psychology professors for interviews. But when I mention that I want the information so I can become a better card counter, my phone calls and emails go unanswered. Finally, I have some success when I contact Lumosity.com, the subscription website that trains people to improve their brains. I send a list of questions and get answers from Dr. Joe Hardy, VP of Research and Development.

I want to know how the brain handles multiple tasks at the same time because this is what I need help with at the blackjack table. I begin by keeping the running count, adjust it for true count, then make adjustments to basic strategy using index plays; then I make the decision to hit, stand, split, double, or take insurance. In between hands I review the count and adjust my betting. This is a lot to do all at once. But Hardy immediately upends my expectations.

"The brain does not generally process demanding cognitive tasks simultaneously," he emails me. "Rather, the brain switches rapidly between tasks, which is a costly process that uses valuable energy and processing power."

This confirms what I notice while playing. When I'm at the table, in the middle of a shoe, and I'm asked a question, perhaps by the dealer or a cocktail waitress, I have to switch from a data mode to a social mode. To do this, I first secure the count in my head before I speak. This does take energy and I can remember feeling the brain switching from one task to another. One trick I use to overcome this transition (although I've never admitted it to Bill) is that I'll keep the count on my fingers as I answer a question. I use my right hand, held palm down, for a positive count and my left for negative counts. If the count is over five I place my hand palm up, meaning that it is five plus however many fingers I extend.

"This task-switching process relies on the strength of our executive function, which is supported by the activity of the prefrontal cortex," Hardy writes. "The prefrontal cortex is involved in planning, impulse control, willpower, and abstract thinking."

It always helps me to relate the multiple activities involved in card counting to other tasks that I've mastered. So I ask Hardy about this. He replies: "Many activities involve task-switching and executive function, such as driving, playing the piano, planning your day, and telling stories."

Hardy's comparison to driving is interesting for several reasons. First, I've been doing it so long that many aspects of driving are performed automatically. For example, when driving a manual shift car, I never think about the individual steps involved in shifting—pressing in the clutch, moving the gear lever, letting out the clutch—I only think, "It's time to shift." This leaves my brain uncluttered for higher functions such as route planning or avoiding an erratic driver. At the blackjack table, I need to make basic strategy completely automatic. Then, my brain is better able to keep the count and make betting decisions.

When a person is nervous or under pressure, how does this affect these skills?

"As we've seen, multitasking is demanding on the brain," Hardy explains. "Additional stressors, like being nervous or under pressure, add more demands to the system, potentially reducing performance. Multiple studies show that stress significantly affects decision-making and interferes with memory formation and retrieval."

I feel like I'm really getting somewhere now in understanding what I've been going through over the past months. I realize that if "stress significantly affects decision-making" I could be making a lot of mistakes I'm unaware of. I think back to Bill's comment that you only need to make two mistakes per hour to give the edge back to the casino. I also recall, when I wrote *Free Throw: 7 Steps to Success at the Free Throw Line*, world champion free-throw shooter Dr. Tom

Amberry told me that there is at least a 10 percent drop-off between practicing free throws and game or tournament conditions.

But when I ask Hardy if there is a drop-off between practicing a skill, such as card counting, and performing under pressure I get a disappointing—though somewhat understandable—answer. "NA—we aren't experts in card counting and cannot speak to this topic." The terse tone reminds me that gambling is a loaded subject and card counting is often thought to be illegal or cheating. But, to be fair, he's a scientist and if he doesn't know the answer he's not about to speculate.

I ask him if there are good exercises for practicing card counting. Again, the disapproving tone, but he does offer a suggestion. "While we are not experts in card counting, the best exercises for your brain are new challenges that use different parts of your brain and increase in difficulty as you improve on tasks."

Hardy also refuses to answer questions about which Lumosity exercises would help me count cards. And when I ask how long it will take to improve, I again get the dreaded "NA" response. He only adds, "This will differ from person to person." *Yes*, I think sadly. *Bill likes to tell me about MIT students he trained in six weeks. For me it's been so much longer.*

When asked when it is best to practice, Hardy's answer is more helpful.

"One of our studies presented at the Entertainment Software and Cognitive Neurotherapeutics Society meeting in 2011 examined cognitive performance peak times of day while performing cognitive tasks. In an analysis of over 170,000 Lumosity users, we found that on average, people performed better at working memory and attention tasks in the morning, but performed better at creative tasks, such as math (problem solving) and verbal fluency, later in the day.

"These results could have implications for the optimal time to perform certain tasks." For students, he said, it could make a difference in what time to take different classes, particularly if you performed better at creative classes, such as English, in the afternoons. I thought of the schedule we usually keep in Las Vegas: up early and hit the tables before noon. Now I realize that not only are my technical skills better, and my memory and brain is working better then, but the tables are empty and the table limits are lower. That's an attractive combination.

After my email interview with Dr. Hardy, I buy a one-month subscription to Lumosity. When I begin playing games on the website, it makes me wish I had been doing it long ago. I can clearly feel my brain switching between tasks, almost as if it is picking up and moving a heavy object. I alternate my Lumosity exercises with practicing card counting both on my computer and with real cards.

Meanwhile, back in my real life, the executive functions of my brain are handling some stressful conditions. There are looming job cuts at my company, my car breaks down, my son is struggling to find a job, and to top it off, I am seated on the jury of a murder trial. Two eighteen-year-olds are accused of stabbing a transient to death because they mistakenly thought he was a pedophile from a local sex offender's shelter. It's a sudden immersion in a dark world of death and ruined lives.

Suddenly, I feel depressed and overwhelmed. For years I tried to solve all such problems myself. But a few years ago, in a similar frame of mind, I found it beneficial to speak with a professional.

I call my health plan provider, thinking it might help me if I can talk with a counselor while on lunch break at the courthouse. Instead, they make a full-on office appointment with a therapist. When I arrive for the appointment several days later, and the therapist listens to my tale of woe, she surprises me by suggesting, "Maybe you have adult ADD."

In my mind, I am just going through a rough patch. But to a trained professional I may have a recognizable psychological condition. Still, her comment connects with many things I've been aware of for some time. I begin to research ADD and take different online quizzes and surveys. Sure enough, the questions match my learning problems and shed light on my slow progress at card counting. Specifically, people with ADD have difficulty focusing on detailed tasks for long periods of time. They make mistakes while trying to rapidly process incoming data. Perhaps trying to learn card counting has unearthed the cause of my nagging learning, listening, and memory problems.

You can't research ADD without very quickly learning a lot about a raft of new wonders sometimes called neuroenhancers. While I've been a lifelong fan of the neuroenhancer caffeine, I soon discovered that college kids prefer a so-called "smart pill," Adderall, often prescribed for ADD. A close cousin is Provigil, which, according to Margaret Talbot in the *New Yorker* article *Brain Gain*, was used by poker player Paul Phillips to boost his performance and sustain his attention during grueling tournaments.

"Within six months, he had won $1.6 million at poker events— far more than he'd won in the previous four years," Talbot writes. "Adderall not only helped him concentrate; it also helped him resist the impulse to keep playing losing hands out of boredom. In 2004, Phillips asked his doctor to give him a prescription for Provigil, which he added to his Adderall regimen. He took between two hundred and three hundred milligrams of Provigil a day, which, he felt, helped him settle into an even more serene and objective state of mindfulness; as he put it, he felt 'less like a participant than an observer—and a very effective one.'"

I am tempted to continue down this road and get a prescription for Adderall to see if it helps my card counting—and my psychological state in general. But, after pondering this issue for several days, I back away. For one thing, ADD seems like the newest, fashionable psychological condition, a way to explain away poor performance. For another thing, I want to master this difficult game unassisted.

Perhaps in the future I will explore these drugs as a way to further boost my winnings. For now, though, I have a new count and, thanks to Professor Memory, a better idea of the mental hurdles I am facing. What I need are a few more weeks of practice, a reality check, and a session in a real casino.

Chapter 18

A Peak Experience

**"Moments of exhilaration and clarity and awareness, the
click that tells you the shot is good before you know it is good."**
—**Adam Smith,** *Powers of Mind*

The closest real casino to my house is Pechanga,
about eighty miles away in the mountain town of
Temecula. It's where I won $360 when I went there with
my father months ago. This test run will show if it helps
my accuracy now that I have adjusted the Knock Out count to avoid
using negative numbers. Most of all, I just want to test my skills,
to see if I can keep the count come hell or high water. Or, more
specifically, come cocktail waitresses or talkative dealers.

Since it's a long way to go just to play blackjack, I call a friend of
mine, Ken, who lives nearby and ask him to play golf. Ken is curious about card counting and asks if he can watch me play. He's an
opera singer, and a tournament bridge player. But I doubt he could
be a card counter since he could never fly under the radar. He's six

feet six inches tall and weighs 330 pounds. Not only that but, to him, life is a performance. He wants to impress everyone he meets. As soon as I agree to let him accompany me, I regret my offer since it will be yet one more distraction. Still, we agree to meet at the casino along with another golf buddy, Frank, who also wants to watch me play. Now I have an audience that will triple the shame if I crash and burn.

When I've talked with my friends about this book project, they show a lot of curiosity about card counting and many of them say they want to learn. Others who already know how to play blackjack say they want to move to the next level and start counting cards. Some even request information about what books to read or what sites to visit. But after a while, I've realized that few, if any, ever follow through. The task is just too daunting, the risks too high. When I realize this it gives me pride in how far I have come. But it also makes me wonder why I pushed on when so many others didn't even take the first step.

It's early morning when Frank and I reach Pechanga. As luck would have it, Ken is pulling in to the parking garage at the same time. We all walk into the casino and stroll into an area that features about eight two-deck tables with $25 table minimums.

I find an open table with an excitable dealer from the Philippines. Frank sits on one side of me and Ken dwarfs me on the other. I buy in for $300 and get twelve green chips.

"You guys have players' cards?" the pit boss asks. He's all business, a tall guy, black hair combed back.

"We're not playing," Ken says, his operatic voice filling the room. "We're going to let Mr. Reed win all the money."

"You want a card?" the pit boss asks me. "You get great benefits."

"No," I tell him. "I don't want my wife to know I'm here. She thinks I have a problem." This is a quick way of deflecting such requests that I've learned from Bill. It usually works because it matches the self-denial typical of many gamblers: "Problem? What problem? I don't have a problem."

But it doesn't cut any ice with this pit boss. He nods, not buying it, and slowly turns away.

I push out a single bet. The dealer gives me a 5 and a 6 for 11 and deals herself a 4. I double and she gives me a 7 for 17. Meanwhile, she gets a 10 then an 8 to bust. Textbook. But according to the Knock Out counting system, the count is now plus 8, not high enough to raise my bets. (Now that I've adjusted the Knock Out to avoid negative numbers, I have to get to plus 10 to raise my bets.) Two hands later, the count climbs into positive territory with a plus 11. I raise my bet to $50 and win again. The count continues to climb, and I force myself to push out yet another chip. Now my bet is at $75.

The dealer gives me a pair of 7s against her 6. I split the 7s and get a 2 on one hand and a 10 on the other. I stand on one hand and double the other. Now I have $225 on the table. She pulls a 5 for 11, which is usually the kiss of death because the dealer often follows with a picture card for a 21. Not this morning. She gets a 2, then a 3, for 15. We're all holding our breath. As the card turns, I see a flash of color and, yes, it's a picture card. She busts. And I win $225 on that hand alone.

Now, I think, *what's the count?* I search around in my brain for the count. Is it plus 10 or plus 11? I've lost the count. And if I'm off by one I'm risking my money without having a mathematical advantage. I pull my bets back to $25 and coast out the rest of the shoe, winning a few more hands.

"Color me up," I tell the dealer at the end of the shoe, pushing my chips forward. The pit boss turns and scans my chips with a cold eye. Then, he supervises the payout, making a note of the total.

"You got great cards," Ken says as we walk to the cage. "I guess I just brought you good luck."

He brought me good luck? I stop and turn to him. "Lucky? So you would know when to raise your bets? You'd know when to double and split?"

"No. I'm just saying—"

I look up at his big face and drop my voice. "If I wasn't counting, I'd have made about $100 on that shoe. Instead—" I open my hand and show him the $500 chip along with a black $100 chip and the green $25. "I got my $300 buy-in back and won $325."

Frank, who is always the peacemaker, shakes his head. "Great playing," he says. "But it was kind of a blur. I don't really know what you did."

"The count climbed steadily through the first two hands," I say, calming down. "Then, when I had my maximum bet out, I got a double and a split and won them all. The point is, I had big money out there when I had an advantage—and it paid off."

"Okay," Frank says, not really understanding. To him it was a flurry of cards that had little significance. His confusions suddenly show me how much I've learned over the past ten months. I feel a bit like Bill when he explained card counting to me on our first trip to Las Vegas.

We head out to the golf course and tee off. Unfortunately, my swing doesn't match my blackjack. I'm spraying the ball all over the damn course. It's probably because my mind is back in the casino. On the one hand I'm pleased with the win and glad I kept the count long enough to make money. But I know that the best opportunities are near the end of the deck. I need to keep the count all the way through to really maximize my advantage. If I can do that here, what will happen next week in Biloxi? I can't wait to find out.

Then, as my excitement gradually diminishes, I remember something Frank said back in the casino, just after I left the table carrying a fist full of chips.

"The pit boss was really watching you," he said. Reviewing my mental footage of the situation I realize he was right. And, looking at it from the pit boss's point of view, I must have had "card counter" written all over my face.

Chapter 19

Confidence Builder

"You'll never win if you're playing with scared money."
—Blackjack proverb

'm having breakfast with Bill and Father Andy in a restaurant overlooking the Gulf of Mexico, in Biloxi, Mississippi, on a beautiful, blustery spring morning. The restaurant is high up on stilts so storm surges can pass underneath. Sunlight is streaming through the windows and outside, across the beach, the wind is blowing the tops off the white caps. Our waitress calls me "Sugar" as she sets down a plate of beignets and a steaming mug of coffee.

And then this pleasant scene is suddenly ruined. I look at my email and see I have an alert from my bank saying my account is overdrawn.

We've had a lot of expenses lately and don't have enough to cover the mortgage. And that's when it hits me—the $2,000 in my pocket for this blackjack trip would have prevented the overdraft.

My wife would kill me if she knew I was playing blackjack with the mortgage money.

I'm ruminating on this crisis when Bill says, "We have to do something about your losses."

My losses! Now my mood is going from bad to worse. *What about yours?* I've seen Bill lose $2,000 in ten minutes. Still, I know what Bill's talking about. The only times I've won since I arrived two days ago is when I walk into a lucky shoe and win using basic strategy.

I'm stuck.

"Let me tell you something," Bill says. "I'd been playing for a few years and I never won a lot. Then, when I first met the MIT guys, they watched me play. They told me, 'Your play is perfect. But the reason you aren't winning is because you've got to get your bets out there to maximize your advantage. That way, when you spread, say, from one to five, and win the hand, it's like you're winning five hands.'

"Listen," Bill continues. "If you flat bet, you'll never turn a profit. And in the long run, when the count is high, you will win more hands than you lose."

"I know you're right but I can't do it, because . . ." My bounced mortgage check is very much on my mind. But I don't want to be a whiner.

"Why not?"

"It scares me." I look at Father Andy for support. He smiles, agreeing, but opts not to join the discussion.

"What are you scared of?"

"Losing money. I don't have a lot and I don't want to lose it."

Bill looks at me sharply. "If you're playing with scared money, you shouldn't be playing."

"I want to play. But I just don't want to lose."

"Then you have to learn to spread your bets when you get a high count. Come on," he says finishing his coffee. "You need a confidence builder."

We walk outside and head over to the Beau Rivage, where I've been staying the past few nights. As we walk, I think back to how I flew into New Orleans two days ago, picked up a rental car, and headed for Biloxi. I hadn't been to New Orleans since before Hurricane Katrina and I was curious to see what it looked like after the storm. From the interstate, it all looked like typical, safe, corporate America. But then I took an off-ramp to a nearby McDonald's for a cup of coffee. As I stepped out of the car, I looked around and saw a creepy, dystopian landscape. Across the street was a low, brick office park, completely deserted, with weeds cracking the asphalt and a big "For Lease" sign plastered across blank, staring windows. Behind me was a shopping mall, the parking lot empty, with only one fast-food joint still in business. Seeing this churned up memories of TV news footage of stranded families on rooftops as President Bush assured us everything was under control.

The drive from New Orleans to Mississippi, through bayous and swamps, took about an hour. As I headed south off the interstate toward Biloxi, it almost looked like the freeway would dump me straight into the Gulf of Mexico. But then the off-ramp circled over the beach and nearly into the lobby of Beau Rivage, where I was staying. When I called to make my reservation a week earlier, the clerk, in a syrupy Southern accent, looked at my players' card account and let out a pleased little gasp.

"Oh, yes," she said. "I'm happy to say, we'll be able to take care of your entire stay."

This comp racket is an unforeseen bonus of my card-counting adventure.

I checked in and requested a room overlooking the Gulf. Up on the twenty-fifth floor, I watched the sun set through gathering clouds. The forecasters predicted rain for the next two days.

Bill warned me that "The Beau," as he calls it, gets very busy on Sunday nights. Sure enough, there was hardly an empty seat at a blackjack table, let alone a chance to play alone, which I learned through a quick walk-through of the casino. So I investigated the Hard Rock next door. That was nuts too. I was itching to play, so I headed out into the night.

The Grand Biloxi, down at the far end of the peninsula, certainly didn't have the class of the Beau. Before Katrina it was the biggest casino in the area. But the hurricane picked up a section of the massive building and moved it several blocks away. Now, it was like they had just given up on the place. The decorations were faded and shopworn and, as I sat down at an open table, I noticed there were cigarette burns in the green felt and stains from spilled drinks.

I bought in for $300 and played one hand head-up against the dealer, a middle-aged bearded man who told me, "It's lucky you can't hear the voices in my head." It's not hard to agree with a statement like that.

The count never got high but, using little more than basic strategy, and winning several doubles, I went up about $275. I was tempted to quit but I decided to boost my winnings even further. One shoe later I walked away dead even.

Back in my hotel room, I stared out at the night and heard rain spatting against the window. Flashes of lightning gave stroboscopic glimpses of the churning waves out in the Gulf. Looking at my reflection in the glass, all I could think was, "Why oh why didn't I walk away when I was ahead?" I could have slept on a win, no matter how modest.

Many blackjack books discuss the fine art of knowing when to walk away from the table. I like what Lance Humble recommends in *The World's Greatest Blackjack Book* when he says that, if you lose three big hands in a row, it's time to leave. However, other experts say it simply doesn't matter when you quit, unless you intend to stop playing blackjack forever. After all, they say, the life of a professional blackjack player is really just one long session.

The next morning Bill and Father Andy arrived, escaping their Midwestern city just before another snowstorm hit. Here in New Orleans it was a humid 65 degrees with light rain.

It had been a while since I talked with Father Andy and I was struck again by how quiet and thoughtful he was. I could picture him in his clerical collar saying Mass.

On the drive, we all agreed to each kick in $2,000 and play out of a mutual bankroll of $6,000. This time we'll split the winnings evenly. I found that I was eager to prove myself by playing on my own.

We spent the rest of the day going from casino to casino only to find that the tables were full or that the games weren't worth playing. There were seven casinos in Biloxi, all within two miles of each other, but only two were consistently promising—the Grand and the Beau. Meanwhile, we dropped off Father Andy at different casinos, where he played video poker. So it amounted to a whole lot of short drives, long walks, and phone calls to coordinate meeting times and places.

We reach the Beau just as I finish reviewing the beginning of the trip in my memory. Now, I am going to have the confidence builder Bill promised back at breakfast. Inside the casino, we walk toward the only open blackjack table where the dealer is a short, pugnacious cracker with a face that looks like a plate full of grits. He glances at us with an arrogant, disinterested look on his face as we settle on the open stools. He sees guys like us every day and he's not the least bit impressed. We're just a couple of shitheads who are going to throw their money away.

"How're you?" Bill asks.

"Doin' fine," the dealer drawls, looking away as he reaches for the stacked two decks of cards and shuffles. I'd been hoping for an easy session at a $25 table. But the only open table is this one with a $50 minimum. So, rather than building my confidence, I'm way out of my comfort zone. And then Bill's words come back to me and I wonder if the cards can really sense that my money is scared? Or is it the dealer? Or the gambling universe that senses my fear?

"Buy in for five," Bill says.

I lay $500 on the felt and put two chips on each hand. I hold my breath. At this rate, I can only lose five hands.

Which is exactly what I do.

"Take out another two," Bill orders.

My head is reeling. But I take out two hundred more and get another eight green chips.

I lose two more hands. And I take out another $200.

I've been at the table less than five minutes and I'm down $700. And even this wiseass dealer is beginning to feel the pain. Out of my peripheral vision I see two guys approach the table, wanting to jump in. But they sense that a battle is in progress and hang back. Then they see what's happening and watch in quiet horror.

On the next hand I catch an 11 against the dealer's 8. But I have no chips to double with. Bill stands up and digs $200 out of his pocket and throws them on the table since, on this trip, we are playing out of a mutual bankroll. I take the chips and double.

And lose.

Bill throws out three hundred more. The room is spinning around me. I can't seem to catch my breath.

The dealer looks at the money on the table but doesn't touch it. "You know guys," the dealer drawls. "Sometimes it's best just to take a walk."

Bill ignores him. He says to me: "A hundred on each hand."

We're down $1,100 and he's telling me to *raise* my bets?

I feel like I'm in a vortex devoid of time and space, just watching my money being sucked into a whirlpool in the center of the table. Any thoughts of keeping the count are long gone. The guys waiting to play are watching my money disappear, and staring as an improbable—but all too familiar—sequence of cards appear. I see my hands push out four more chips on each hand. And finally—*finally*—I win them both.

"One fifty on each hand," Bill says.

I just won my first hands, and now Bill wants me to raise my bets even more! I obey and win two more hands. I keep my bets out there and split the next two hands. The cut card appears and I play and win the last two hands. A few seconds later the shoe is over and I scoop up the chips and stagger away from the table.

We're near the cashier when Bill gets in my face. "See? If we had left after the first couple of hands, that could have been a really ugly $1,400 loss. But we hung in there. You had a monster count so we kept the chips on the table. And we walked away losing only $700. Do you see?"

"Yeah, I see. But it wasn't exactly the confidence booster I needed."

"I guess not," Bill says, relaxing. "Your hands were really shaking. Come on, we've got to go get Father Andy."

We find the priest seated happily in front of a "good machine" he found over at another casino, Margaritaville. It's one of the new casinos that sprouted up, growing like a big old weed out of the mud after the floodwaters of Katrina receded. Since Father Andy is happy, we look around and find an open blackjack table. The dealer is a tall, friendly, redheaded woman with a sweet Mississippi accent.

Bill sits down and the game starts. I practice counting as he plays. I'm so relieved not to be in the hot seat. I see that the count is climbing. Bill spreads from one to two units on each hand, then three and four. By the end of the first shoe he's won $375, cutting my loss in half. He is ready to play another shoe when a new dealer appears. He's a thick-necked good old boy who looks like he moonlights as a bouncer. After he shuffles the cards, he puts the cut card right in the middle of the two decks. He's cutting out an entire deck! This is horrible penetration.

"You're kidding, right?" Bill says to the guy.

"What?" the big lug asks with mock innocence.

Bill stares him down. "Okay. I get it." He picks up his chips and we leave.

"They must have seen me upstairs and sent in a different dealer," Bill says.

We find Father Andy and head out. I'm catching a plane in about three hours so we only have time for one more session. And I'm still looking for that confidence builder.

We head back to the Grand. It's the middle of the afternoon but all the tables are full. Father Andy and I stand off to the side while I see Bill approach the pit boss. He begins negotiating with him in his polite but insistent way. Moments later, Bill rejoins us.

"I told him if he opened a $25 table we would all play," Bill says to us. I see the pit boss scurrying around in the background. Father Andy reacts with a small smile that seems to say, "I know you're not serious." We stand and watch as the pit boss pulls a woman off of a Mississippi Stud game that no one is playing. The woman and the pit boss break open and shuffle multiple packs of cards. It's a laborious process of counting the cards, pulling out jokers, stacking the decks, and shuffling. Finally, they are ready for us.

As we sit down we see it is only a $25 game, but the stakes are high enough to keep the other players away. They all flock to the safety—and sociability—of the $5 minimum tables.

The dealer is an older woman whose brown hair has somehow held off the usual invasion of gray. She has a strong, intelligent face and I can sense right away that she likes us and is glad to have someone to talk with. Bill keeps up a steady patter with her and Father Andy watches quietly. After my initiation by fire at the $50 table, I find I am relaxed and able to keep the count here, betting one hand against the dealer as the count edges up and down as slowly as the tide out in the Gulf.

By the end of the first shoe I've built up a nice $250 win. But the count is high and I wait for the signal from Bill. Sure enough, he tells me to spread to two hands and raise my bets to $75 on each. I play three hands this way—for a total of six bets—and lose most of them. My winnings are all gone.

On the next shoe I gradually lose most of my chips. I hover near extinction and then build my way back to even. On the next shoe, we watch as the nice dealer lady puts the cut card close to the end of the deck. Bill gives me that look that means deep penetration.

I'm up a little, down a little for most of the shoe. But toward the end, Bill gives me the signal to spread to two hands and raise my bets to $75. I brace myself for another loss. But this time the cards fall in my favor. I win nearly eight large bets in a row. A few minutes later, I walk away with a $625 win.

"I was two chips away from tapping out," I say to Father Andy as we walk to the cage.

"Yeah," he laughs, rolling his eyes in acknowledgment. "That was kind of wild."

"Were you praying?" I ask.

My question jolts him and snaps him back into his official role.

"It doesn't work like that," he answers carefully.

"You better tell the guys that in the NFL," I say. "They think God is on their side if they pray in the locker room."

Father Andy smiles and starts to speak, but thinks better of it. It's a complicated subject and he knows that a casino cashier's window isn't the best place to discuss it.

We sit in a coffee shop and settle up. As Bill meticulously adds up our wins and losses, he says, "You see how that last shoe worked? We were up a little, down a little, and then we made all our money on the last six or seven hands."

"Yeah, but before that, we lost the big hands."

Bill stops writing and looks up. His eyes are steady and he has a trace of impatience. He speaks slowly.

"If you want to beat this game you have to put your money on the table."

"Bill, I know, it's just that—" I stop, thinking of the old expression that you should never apologize, never explain. "I got an email from my bank. I'm overdrawn on my mortgage. I can't afford to lose."

Instead of getting sympathy from him, I get a lecture.

"I told you before, if you're playing with scared money, you shouldn't be playing." He holds my gaze. Then he returns to total up the money. A few minutes later, we pull out our bankrolls and even the score. After two days of playing, I've only won about $200.

On the way to the airport I think back to that last session, to those final hands. The remark about "scared money" still burns. But, I also feel that something has changed. At a deep level, I think I can accept the risk necessary to make money. I don't know for sure, but I feel that I may have reached a turning point. I might have finally gotten over the hump.

A few days after I get home I get an email from Father Andy and I love the way it begins.

"This morning, in preparation for our upcoming parish mission on Catholic mystics, I was reading Thomas Merton, my favorite monk and mystic. I came across these lines and thought of Bill:

"According to the Christian mystical tradition, one cannot find one's inner center and know God there as long as one is involved in the preoccupations and desires of the outward self. Penetration into the depth of our being is, then, a matter of liberation from the ordinary flow of consciousness and half-consciousness sense impressions, but also and more definitely from the unconscious drives and clamoring of inordinate passion."

The phrase "penetration into the depth of our being" strikes a chord. As I read the words I realize that "deep penetration," the words that Bill stressed so early in my blackjack education, also apply to his consciousness and perhaps to his state of mind as he plays blackjack.

And, as I think of this, a picture of Bill jumps into my mind. I see him sitting at a blackjack table, watching the flow of cards with an almost mystical understanding of the math behind them, and a love and appreciation of the system he uses to bring order and, ultimately, victory to seeming chaos.

A short time later I get a text message from Bill, which is an interesting counterpart to Father Andy's rumination about mystics. Bill simply writes: "Up $4,200 in Biloxi. Good trip."

Chapter 20

Blackjack Fortune-Teller

"Standard deviation is just another name for luck."
—Professional gambler

Jaacob Bowden, a golf pro friend of mine, sends me an email saying he is working with a business consultant to build up his website on swing-speed training. He says this consultant helps all kinds of people in many different areas.

"You should do a session with her about blackjack," he says. "Maybe she could find out why you've been losing."

Jaacob was referring to a recent trip I took to Las Vegas where I took some brutal losses. Even Bill was shaking his head in disbelief, wondering why the cards were so bad.

I decide to call Jaacob's business consultant, a woman who lives in the San Fernando Valley near Los Angeles. But instead of asking her about my blackjack performance, I broach another issue: I ask her to help my son who has just graduated from college and is struggling to find a job.

Over the phone she tells me: "I can help him with his resume, his goal creation, and his interview skills. But if you want, I can also do other things."

"Um, what other things are we talking about?" I ask.

"I can help people on other levels."

"Okay, what do you do?"

"It's hard to describe," she says, laughing pleasantly. "I seem to be able to sense people's energy and help them remove blocks."

It's interesting that she brings this up at this time. While much of this past year has been dominated by blackjack trips, in other areas, my thinking is going through a radical shift. It started when a man who had read my horse-racing thriller, *The Marquis de Fraud*, contacted me and asked me to write a book for him. He said he had already worked with authors on other subjects and wanted to send me some books so I could familiarize myself with his thinking.

One of the books was about a man who was killed crossing the street but came back from the dead with a detailed description of heaven. This piqued my interest and led me to read the incredible *Life after Life* by Raymond A. Moody Jr., MD. I also watched a documentary about how Dr. Helen Schucman, a professor at Columbia University, in New York, heard a voice in her head. She took "dictation" from this voice and it became the book *A Course in Miracles*.

All this reading makes me realize how many factors affect us that aren't recognized or proved by science. Of course religion and science have always been at odds. In fact, in my upbringing my mother read us the Bible while my father argued that science holds all the answers. But even outside of religion there are phenomena such as extrasensory perception that can't be explained. Even simple intuition has produced many great ideas and inventions.

So what does all this have to do with blackjack?

I have been so focused on the count, the math, and the cards, that I have overlooked all the other factors that are at play when you sit down at a blackjack table. Most gamblers just bundle all this into the general category of luck. But card counters, such as Bill, know that luck doesn't exist. However, Bill does accept the importance of elements such as confidence. And even the great blackjack player Ken Uston said that belief in superstition was almost inevitable. In his book *One Third of a Shoe*, Uston writes about a brief time in the 1970s in Atlantic City, NJ, when card counting was allowed by the casinos. He organized a team and they played almost nonstop for two weeks and won $40,000.

"I admit to paying homage to occasional lapses of superstition," Uston writes. "Once, while playing with Team #1 about four years ago, I experienced several losing sessions in a row. This, of course, happens to all of us. The next morning before leaving to play I put on some Old Spice aftershave lotion. My next session was a dramatic winner. For the next several weeks I doused myself with this lotion without fail each time. If I went out the door and remembered that I forgot the aftershave lotion I returned for it. The skeptic would reply, 'Attitudes can't affect the cards you get.' True, but I don't know a single successful blackjack professional who isn't a believer in positive attitude for whatever reason."

A positive attitude is a combination of many different things, including ability, confidence, energy, and opportunity—to name a few. But there are deeper factors at work too. I begin to wonder if there is something buried in my subconscious blocking my energy at the blackjack table, some deeply held belief, perhaps, in the sinfulness of gambling that brings my unexpected losses.

A few days later, I do a Google search on the words "intuition" and "blackjack." Sure enough, I find a blog post on Blackjackinfo.com from "Gamblor" that talks about a study in which bridge players can sense when a computer has shuffled the cards rather than a human. Even more significantly, in one study, they found that the players' bodies reacted physically to the "unnatural" flow of cards before their conscious mind signaled the feedback. Gamblor concludes: "I think there is no doubt that the subconscious mind does a huge amount of processing behind the scenes, and the conscious mind is only the tip of the iceberg."

Another hit from my Google search looks interesting. I find a blog post written by Dan Liss's MagicAwakenings.com, where he writes: "It is still possible for intuition to have a rule alongside the logical rules of blackjack. It is a game where intuition and logic will battle. There were times when I just felt like I should take a card, and other times where the traditional rules served well."

Bill would be horrified by this approach. He has always warned me not to become a "hunch player." Still, I believe that there is something here for me to learn. As Liss writes: "Being aware of energies in a casino is an interesting experience. I noticed changes in energy with dealers too. Even though they are all trained and they all act professionally, there is definitely a difference."

On Liss's website I notice that he offers a variety of services, from consultations to past-life readings. I opt for a one-hour consultation for $100. I write out a list of questions and call him at the agreed-upon hour.

On the phone from his home in Colorado, Liss sounds very normal—not like some gypsy fortune-teller. He is friendly and thoughtful and has a patient, warm voice. I'm very sensitive to people's voices. For me, it's a way to get to know someone. Right away, I like him and sense a connection. He says he began his career in marketing, then moved to advertising, and then became a magazine editor. Along the way, he found he could help people solve their problems on many different levels. (This echoes the words of Jaacob's business consultant.) As an experiment, he began to document his results and, once convinced, he began to charge for his services and pursue spiritual work full-time.

I tell Liss about my blackjack playing, and my book, and ask the first question on my list: "I'm taking a lot of losses. Do you think I should continue playing blackjack?"

Liss answers, "Sometimes, when you get blocked, and you lose, it makes you ask if there is something else to the process and you explore other areas such as destiny. Your destiny is to pursue other thoughts and insights uniquely available to you and to share them with other people."

I take this to mean that even though I haven't made as much money as I would like, the losses force me to dig deeper and possibly enrich the book I'm writing. Okay. I can see that.

Next, I tell Liss how my mother was deeply religious and I've wondered if she instilled a sense of guilt that is undercutting my ability to win.

"If you believe that getting money playing blackjack is not as honorable as being, for example, an insurance salesman, that belief will undermine you," he answers. "But keep in mind that you are still honoring your Creator because you are trying to become the best blackjack player you can be. Then, you can then take pride in your workmanship and your pride will overcome your guilt."

Liss's answers inspire me to open up and then I hear myself ask a question that isn't even on my list.

"Do you think it's wrong to pray to win at blackjack?"

"You can pray for almost anything," Liss quickly answers. "In all of our endeavors, whenever we pray, all we are asking for is a little divine help if we can get it. And when we do this we are focusing our intentions. You are focusing your energy on being more successful in blackjack."

But, I ask him, how do I deal with the fear I feel at the table?

"You have to understand that love and fear are opposites. So if you are betting, say, $5,000, and this suddenly strikes you as a lot of money, fear comes in. And with fear comes greed. But if you say to yourself, 'I love this game,' you will lose fear and greed and play at a higher level.

"There is a natural rhythm to everything," he continues. "There is a rhythm with the dealer, you have your own rhythm, and you are following the rhythm as you play."

After I hang up I realize that I haven't been paying attention to my intuition or my natural rhythm. And I've been playing at a level that is way over my head, where the fear exists. I've ignored the love of the game for the pursuit of the money.

Next week, the automotive website I work for is sending me to St. Louis to spend a weekend in a car dealership to research a new program it is developing. Preparing for the trip, I am supposed to be boning up on my product information about different car models. Instead, I spend a lot of time trying to find if there is a good two-deck game in the area. The casino opportunities look promising. This is my chance to find my own rhythm and make this game my own.

Chapter 21

Tapping an Inside Source

"Part of it went on gambling, and part of it went on women. The rest I spent foolishly."
—George Raft

For this book I really wanted to interview a dealer or pit boss from the casino side but I'm having troubling finding anyone willing to talk with me. Then, a golden opportunity falls into my lap.

When I arrive in St. Louis, I go to a car dealership to answer car-buying questions and I am assigned to sit at a desk on the dealership's showroom floor. Slowly, I get to know the different salesmen who work around me. One day, I'm in the break room when I get to talking to Stan, one of the car salesmen. He mentions he has only been selling cars for a few years.

"What did you do before this?" I ask.

"Worked for a casino."

"Really?" I say, trying not to seem too interested. "Were you a dealer?"

"Dealer. Pit boss. Casino manager. I pretty much did it all."

Stan is in his forties, dark hair, glasses, a little paunchy with a resemblance to the actor Dan Aykroyd. He ambles around the showroom, his head cocked to one side, an affable, amused look on his face. I can picture him in a casino, dressed in a suit, standing in the blackjack pit and shooting the breeze with the dealers and players.

"How'd you get into the casino business?"

He shrugs. "I hung around the horse track since I was kid. Then I was a dealer . . . Worked my way up through the casino system."

"Did you supervise the blackjack tables?"

"Sure. And now my wife's a casino supervisor at one of the casinos down in the south end of town."

It's interesting how some conversations are like two dogs circling each other, warily assessing each other. It's time to go to the next level.

"So, do you play blackjack?"

"Used to."

"Do you count?"

He gives a wary smile. He considers how to respond, then says: "Well, I'm out of practice right now."

Anyone who provides this answer knows what they are talking about. Card counting is almost like a language, you need to use it constantly or your skills diminish.

"So what system do you use?" I put my question in the present tense. He has tried to distance himself from card counting, but I sense he is still involved.

"I use the Hi-Opt 2."

My opinion of him goes up another notch. The Hi-Opt 2 is a difficult two-level count, similar to the Zen count that Bill uses. Instead of adding or subtracting by 1, some of the cards are worth 2 and others are only 1.

"So why don't you play anymore?"

"Everyone knows me in the casinos around here. Besides, I got my ass kicked a lot."

"At blackjack?"

"Craps. I love to play craps."

"But it has a negative expectation."

"I know. But I love the action. There's nothing like a hot craps table."

At this point another salesman walks into the break room and we suspend our conversation.

That night, I go to one of the many St. Louis area casinos with my co-workers. I've been eager to try a different approach to blackjack after my consultation with Dan Liss. I'm going to pay attention to not only the math, but also the energy of the dealers and the other players at the table. I'll focus on the love of the game, not the fear of losing. This, by the way, is often cited as a winning strategy for athletes, particularly golfers and tennis players. They become professionals because they love the game, only to discover that playing their sport for money ruins the fun. Once they change the focus back to a higher level, they find that winning is a by-product.

It's Saturday night and the casino is crazy busy. The Cardinals are in the World Series, and the ball game is blaring from the casino sound system.

Still smarting from my losses in Las Vegas, and because it is so busy, I decide not to play the $25 two-deck game. Instead, I scope out the $10 six-deck games and look for a place I can sit and practice counting. I find a table with an open spot and stand behind it, waiting for the shoe to end. I watch as the dealer makes two five-card 21s in a row.

"He's a house dealer," a guy beside me says.

The dealer hears the comment. "Hey, brother, I can't control the cards."

"You're a house dealer," the guy repeats, challengingly.

The dealer shakes his head. A few hands later the shoe ends so I take a seat and buy in with $200. I have a nice big pile of red chips in front of me. Beside me, the guy is playing black and orange chips on two hands: $100 and $500 a hand.

"I have to quit playing drunk," the guy says to me, sipping a glass of whiskey.

"That's an excellent idea," I reply.

But he doesn't stop. And he also doesn't know how to play. He is missing doubles and is making lots of basic strategy mistakes. Meanwhile, since it is a six-deck game, I decide to use the Knock Out count beginning at plus 10 and plan to increase my bets at plus 26. With so many cards in the shoe I am unsure I can catch good hands. But after one shoe, I win $75. It makes me nervous, though, because the guy next to me is losing thousands of dollars and his mood is turning ugly. I decide to cash out and call it a little confidence-building win.

I find my co-workers at a nearby $10 blackjack table. Among them is a friend of mine who knows I am writing a blackjack book. He's a good basic strategy player, but he hasn't learned to count cards. Instead, he relies on the "progression" system, also known as the martingale betting strategy. When you win a hand, you double the next bet and keep doubling until you lose again. The theory is that you can't lose because eventually you get a big win that pays back all your losses. However, it's a deeply flawed system because long losing streaks occur more often than are commonly thought and most gamblers don't have the bankroll to outlast them. If you were playing roulette, for instance, and betting on red or black for $10, losing only six spins in a row would require the seventh bet to be $640 just to get back to even money.

At one point I ask Stan, the ex-casino guy, about progression bettors.

"Casinos love the progression system," he says, throwing his head back and laughing. "Love, love, love it!"

Meanwhile, back in the casino, my friend is calling the shots for the whole table. And everyone is winning. My friend cashes out with a $125 win and what he feels is confirmation of the progression system.

Back at the car lot the next day, I notice that Stan is eyeing me across the dealership with a knowing twinkle in his eye. I wait for him to walk out front and then I join him at the curb. It's a cool, breezy autumn day. The dealership looks out on a busy freeway and we watch the passing cars as we talk.

"You play last night?" he asks. "After our little chat yesterday I figured that was where you were headed."

"Just one shoe at the $10 tables. I had a small win."

"Nothin' wrong with that," he says, firing up a cigarette.

It is a slow day without a single customer on the lot.

"So how did you like working in the casino?" I ask.

"Oh God, when I was young, single, it was great," he says, rolling his eyes and laughing. "I mean, look at me, I'm not a handsome guy. But the cocktail waitresses . . ." He laughs again. "It was great."

"How much did you make?"

"Four dollars an hour. But with tips it came out to about $25 an hour."

"Why did you learn to count?"

"The casino wanted me to learn so I could spot card counters. But then I started playing on my own. They even sent me out to California to check out the Indian casinos. They wanted me to figure out how to bring in more Asian customers."

"What'd you tell them?"

"Have more Asians live nearby."

"Makes sense."

"It was a great gig. The casino even gave me money to gamble with."

"Sweet."

"I spent a lot of time in the poker rooms. But then I lost it all at the craps table."

"When you were a supervisor, did you have to back off counters?"

"In Missouri, it's illegal to bar card counters. But if I knew a guy was counting, and I didn't like him, I'd wait until he had a big bet out there and then I'd tell the dealer: 'Shuffle up!' They usually got the message and left."

It is an interesting way to frame his answer. "What do you mean, 'If you didn't like him'?"

"If he wasn't tipping the dealer. If he was an asshole. If he was getting greedy."

"How much did you let them win before you shuffled up on them?"

"Depended. If I liked the guy, if they played short sessions, they could get five hundred, a grand maybe, without a hassle. That's not big action for the casino."

"But were the counters really that easy to spot?"

"For me, sure."

"What's the tip-off?"

"Jumping your bets all of a sudden. Taking insurance and winning. Variations from basic strategy."

"But how can they spot that in surveillance? Are the cameras really that good?"

He smiles and pushes the glasses up on his nose. "Let me tell you something. If I was in surveillance, and you put a dollar bill on a blackjack table, I could read the serial number off it."

"How many guys do they have upstairs watching the screens?"

"Where I worked, there were only four guys."

"Watching thirty tables? That's a lot of players to check out. I'm surprised that they could spot a card counter."

"Usually it started with a call from the pit. A supervisor gets a feeling about a player and calls surveillance: 'Hey, watch the guy on table five.'"

"So the surveillance guys know how to count?"

"They enter the cards being played into a computer. If the bet spread matches the count, he's history."

We watch the passing traffic for a few minutes. I am beginning to realize that Stan might have been a sharp supervisor, and an accomplished card counter, but in his heart he is a gambler. I decide to put my theory to the test.

"So, as a player, what was your best day ever?"

"For blackjack?"

"Everything."

"Oh gosh. I had this one day . . ." He smiles at the memory. "I mean, I couldn't lose. It started when I won two grand at craps. Then I took it and won a bundle on pai gow poker. And I finished up at the blackjack tables. By then I was so shit-faced I couldn't see the cards. But I could not lose. All in all I took 'em for $18,000."

"Whoa."

"It was amazing. I could not lose."

"Knowing what you know, you could put together a team, make some real money."

"Sure, I've thought about it. But you need a serious bankroll for that. Besides, the successful teams are really well organized. They fly guys in days before they play. They watch the supervisors to see which ones are paying attention so they know what shifts to play on. They start buying chips and stockpile them. They hire chip runners to finance the players. It's just a whole lot of work."

His voice trails off as he watches a car approach. It slows to a stop. He stubs out his cigarette and begins moving toward the potential customers.

"Besides, there's still one problem." He looks back with a sheepish smile. "I can never pass a craps table. I just can't do it. I love the action."

Stan reaches the car as a middle-aged couple steps out. I can hear his friendly voice: "And how are you folks doing on this fine afternoon?"

From a casino to a car lot—what does that tell you?

That night I go to my first World Series game ever with my blackjack friend. We watch as the Red Sox beat the Cardinals 4 to

2. On the walk back to the car we spot another casino and decide to stop in for a quick session. For most of the day I'd been thinking about what Stan told me: that if he liked some card counters he let them play. That fit with what I read in Ian Anderson's book *Turning the Tables in Las Vegas*. I've read a lot of blackjack books doing research for this project and Anderson is my favorite author on the subject. He describes how he spends a lot of time building relationships with dealers and pit bosses to avoid detection as a card counter. As soon as he sits down at the table, Anderson lays out a small bet for the dealer, saying, "Have I told you about my profit-sharing plan?"

My friend and I sit at a $15 six-deck game. The dealer is a beautiful young woman but she has a difficult time shuffling and stacking all the cards. Once we start to play, on the first three hands I get 20 but end with either a push or a loss. My friend fares even worse.

"I don't like the way this table feels," he says, and he picks up his chips and heads for another table.

The count is climbing and, even though I am down about $100, I sit tight. Then a new dealer comes in, a young African American woman with thick glasses. She is so inexperienced she recounts any hand with an ace to make sure she gets it right. But there is something about her I like. Even though she is inexperienced, she is quiet and smart and is trying really hard. I know she will eventually be a good dealer. Maybe she will work her way up through the system and be a supervisor, like Stan.

After a few hands I put out a $1 bet for her and lose it. The count continues to climb. Finally, the count is so high I double my bet.

And then the fun begins.

It is one of those textbook sessions where everything that is supposed to happen, actually happens. If I get a 14 against a dealer's 4, she has a 10 underneath and draws a face card to bust. At one point, I stand on a 15 against a dealer's 10 and she has a 6 and draws a high card to bust. I even insure one hand and, in fact, she has blackjack. I feel almost like Stan: I can't lose.

I put out another $1 tip for the dealer. She gives me an 11 and so I double for both of us, putting out another $1 chip for her. She gives me a 10 for a 21 and turns her tip into $4. It is the last hand of the shoe.

"I'd like to color up," I tell the dealer.

The pit boss comes over to supervise the payoff.

"You've got a good dealer here," I tell the pit boss.

"That's good to hear," he says, looking over my chips. "She just started."

"Really?" I say, acting surprised. "I couldn't tell."

I look at the young dealer, standing silently beside her boss, and I think I see her smile.

The dealer counts out my chips and I give her an extra $5 tip. I see the eyes of the pit boss dart approvingly toward the red chip. It isn't a lot of money. But it told him that I "get it."

"Thank you, sir," the dealer says as I walk away with a handful of black and green chips.

I find my friend at a nearby table with a sour expression on his face. An old dealer is firing cards at him. Every time the dealer busts he yells, "Hasta la vista!" My friend scoops up a few remaining chips and we head for the cashier.

"I just lost $300 in a hurry," he says. "How'd you do?"

"Up a hundred and thirty. The count got high right after you left."

"Yeah. I knew I should have stayed."

Chapter 22

Breaking Through

"Knowing how to count cards is like having a college degree in your back pocket."
—Bill Palis

head out early one Sunday morning in December, bound for Las Vegas, behind the wheel of the new all-electric luxury car, the Tesla Model S, which I'm test-driving for my automotive website. The freeways are empty and my spirits are high. Five hours later, after a brief stop at Tesla's "superchargers" in Barstow, I reach the airport and see Bill standing at the curb, waiting for me. I suddenly flash back to the first time I saw him here, about a year ago. It's amazing to think how much has happened since then.

I see Bill nod in appreciation as the midnight blue Tesla S slides to a stop at the curb.

"Nice car!" Bill says as I greet him and he puts his bag in the huge trunk. Since the car is all electric, and has no bulky gas motor, there is plenty of storage space both in the front and back. The car's front trunk—the so-called "frunk"—is perfect for hiding my $5,000 bankroll from valet parking attendants.

On the drive from the airport Bill tells me he had to pay for his hotel room for the first time in ten years. I respond by bragging that I am getting comped at the Cosmopolitan for the third time. He looks at me, smiling, and asks, "Is there something you're not telling me about yourself?"

We have a quick lunch in the bar at the Peppermill and set the terms for the trip. We each brought $5,000, and Father Andy is kicking in five grand. Together with some investor money Bill has found, we have a $30,000 bankroll—the most I've ever played out of. As Bill gives me my playing money, counting out hundred-dollar bills, he says, "If anyone saw us now, they would think we were doing a drug deal."

We discuss our playing strategy as we eat. But our brainstorming only serves to make Bill restless. Finally, after wolfing down his food, he can't stand it anymore.

"Let's go play!" he says, jumping to his feet.

We decide to start at the Aria. But as we walk into the casino and start scouting the tables, the only open table we find has a $100 minimum.

"You're up," Bill says, as we approach the table. Behind the chip tray is a tall young man with a barely concealed smirk on his face.

I've been concentrating on learning the indexes that come up most often, such as 16 and 15 against a dealer's 10, and 12 and 13 against a dealer's 2 or 3. Normally, basic strategy calls for hitting 12 and 13 against a dealer's 2. But the card counter knows that when the count is plus 2, it's best to stand on a 12 against a dealer's 2. Not only do I have these indexes to remember, but Bill gives me several advanced plays he says are little known but highly effective. They shall remain secret.

At the Aria, with a $100 black chip on each hand, I feel like I've been thrown into the deep end of the swimming pool. I must have been really nervous because I signal that I want to stand on a 12 against what I think is a dealer's 2.

"Unusual," the dealer smirks and proceeds to hit his hand.

Meanwhile Bill, perhaps in shock, takes a moment to react.

"Why'd you stand?" he asks disgustedly. "You don't stand on a 12!"

I want to say, "But the count is high!" But of course I can't say this in front of the dealer.

"Maybe he knows something we don't," the dealer says, flipping over his next card. He busts and I win the hand. But Bill is clearly agitated. At the end of the shoe Bill stands.

"Okay, that's enough," Bill says.

I pick up my chips and we head for the cage.

"You made at least four errors," Bill says.

"Okay. What were they?"

"For starters, you can't stand with a 12 against 10," Bill says. "That's a basic strategy error."

"But the count was high," I say. "I thought I was supposed to stand on 12 against a dealer's 2 when the count is high."

"The dealer had a 10!" Bill says. "You stood on a 12 against a 10. That's a really bad basic strategy error."

"I did?" I'm completely confused and shaken. I don't know what I saw, but it wasn't a 10. Still, both Bill and the dealer had reacted to it, so I must have been the one who was wrong.

We're at the cage now. I cash in and find I've won $250, which is a huge relief.

"You got away with it because the dealer busted," Bill says. "But you can't be out there making mistakes like that. I mean, come on, it's almost been a whole year and you're still making basic strategy errors."

All of a sudden I feel like I'm back in the stupid club. All the terrible experiences of my childhood come roaring back and my face burns with shame.

"Bill, I don't know what happened," I say. "But I assure you, I won't make that mistake again."

"Okay," he sighs. "Here's what we're going to do. You're going to have to play at the $25 level and only spread to $75. We have Father Andy's money too. We can't risk mistakes like that again."

Bill's right, I've been at this for a full year now and it's time to see results. I push the anger and shame away and focus on the task at hand: becoming a winning player. It's a tough way to start the trip, but I am determined not to let it bother me. It was just one mistake and I got away with it. So I'll just look at it as a cheap way to remind myself to focus and concentrate.

We drive north to the downtown area so Bill can check in at the Nugget, where he again mentions how much he hates actually paying for his room. After he gets settled, he heads downstairs to play in the high-limit area. I split off and head for the D, where Bill was backed off several months ago.

It's Sunday afternoon and when I walk into the casino a wall of pounding music hits me in the face. Huge TV monitors show UFC fighters bloodying their opponents and basketball players slam-dunking. Dancers in bikinis grind away on platforms in the pits and the tables are jammed. But above the main floor, a table is open with a $25 minimum bet. I block out all the negative thoughts, all the self-doubt, and sit down to play. I lay my $500 on the green felt and the dealer shuffles.

The pit boss slides over.

"Want a players' card?"

"No, thanks," I say because, among other things, I already have one. But I don't use it for fear they've got a record of seeing me with

Bill when he was backed off. The pit boss gives me a mild, "Good luck, sir," folds his arms, and watches as the dealer snaps out the cards.

I play two hands of $50 each even though Bill instructed me to drop down to a $25 minimum bet. Halfway through the shoe the count rises and I go to $75 on each hand and catch a blackjack. *Nice.* The count is working. I win a double, and later a split, and when the first shoe ends, I call it quits. After the dealer colors me up, I find I've won $480. With the $500 I bought in with, she pays me $980. The dealer announces the total to the pit boss, who looks from the chips on the table to my face. His eyes sweep over me, filing the memory.

As I walk to the cage, I feel the dull weight of the chips in my hands: one $500 chip and an assortment of blacks and greens. I flash back on another memory from a year ago: cashing in Bill's chips and handing the money over to him. This time, the chips, and the money they represent, are my victory, and at least some of it will go in my pocket.

I text the news of my win to Bill but get no answer. I walk back down Fremont Street in the late afternoon heat and into the smoky noise of the Nugget. There's something desperate about Sunday afternoons in Vegas. Around me gamblers are pounding drinks and shouting over the noise of the music and the din of all these voices. It's like everyone is desperately trying to hold off Monday in hopes that reality will never return.

Looking into the high-limit area I see Bill playing with a determined look on his face. He doesn't see me. I feel vindicated by the $480 win—and a total win of $730 for the afternoon—so I decide to take a break from playing and put some juice in the electric car's battery. I look on my phone app and find a charger nearby. I drive to the Clark County Courthouse plug-in, and walk back to the Nugget along deserted backstreets. In Las Vegas, when you get one or two blocks off the Strip or downtown's Fremont Street, you're in another world. Homeless guys wander idly or slump in doorways.

As I hurry along, I suddenly feel vulnerable as I realize I have almost $4,000 in cash in my pockets.

After dinner, we head over to the Wynn since tables at the other casinos will probably be jammed. Bill buys in for a grand at a $100 table. I sit with him and we both order a Pinot Noir from a gorgeous cocktail waitress in a sequined uniform with a low-cut front and no back. Meanwhile, the cards turn ugly and Bill quickly loses $1,000 worth of black chips.

"That's an expensive glass of wine, Joel," Bill says, reading the name tag on a pit boss who's been watching the slaughter.

Joel smiles sympathetically. "Some nights are like that."

Bill buys in for another grand. And then another. Then, I feel a change coming, as if a different weather pattern is blowing in. As the next shoe begins, an odd sense of calm comes over me. Bill begins to play even with the dealer. I am completely confident in Bill's abilities. It's almost as if I can hear the calculations in Bill's head, the deciphering of what—to most people—is a complete mystery that causes them to call the whole thing luck. I relax, sip my excellent free wine, and wait for the inevitable.

Soon, Bill gets a double and a split, and then a double on one of the splits. He wins them all for a net gain of $600. A short time later, he wins back all his money and goes up $1,300. All this time he seems fearless, almost amused, by the outcome.

"Nice comeback," the pit boss, Joel, says, shaking his head in amazement as the dealer colors up his chips. "I've never seen someone come all the way back like that before."

"I couldn't believe it either," Bill says, laughing. "I guess my luck turned."

Bill is acting like a gambler and the pit boss is buying right into it.

"Can I ask you something, Joel?" Bill says.

"Sure."

"I'm thinking about changing casino hosts. I'm not getting the attention I'd like from my current guy. Would you feel comfortable recommending someone who you think is really good?"

I know right away that Bill is working the pit boss. There's a real art to working someone. Like a good sales job, there actually has to be honesty and respect. Joel actually seems pleased that Bill is tapping him for insider information.

"There's a guy here," Joel says. "His name is Bruce. Great guy. Very popular. In fact, he's in his office over there if you want to meet him."

"Thanks, Joel," Bill says, shaking his hand. "I really appreciate your help."

I loiter nearby as Bill goes into the lush office and meets a middle-aged man with sandy hair and a friendly, open face. From a distance, I hear polite phrases and occasional laughter. I know that Bill is now working Bruce, giving him the first-class treatment. The whole experience, the wine, the comeback win, the cordiality of the casino staff, gives me a warm glow of success.

I realize that I'm learning another valuable lesson. If you have the guts—and the bankroll—to be a black-chip player, you've entered an elite world. The tables are open, the free drinks are better, the cocktail waitresses are stunning, and the pit bosses don't sweat your action. I take a sip of my free wine and think, *Yeah, I could get used to this.*

Bill rejoins me and we sit among the slot machines and order another glass of free wine. Bill just won $1,300, but we'll be damned if we'll actually pay for our wine.

"We're up almost two grand for the day," Bill says. "That's about right. We want to make two grand a day between us. That way, we finish the trip with at least six thou."

Back in my suite, on the twenty-fourth floor of the Cosmopolitan, I go out on the balcony and watch as the Bellagio fountain blasts lighted jets of water into the night. I let my eyes wander over the skyline of the Bellagio, the Eiffel Tower at Paris, the Flamingo, and, in the distance, the Stratosphere. A strange thought grows in my mind. I realize I am looking at the physical manifestation of human greed—the greed of the casino owners who are willing to ruin the lives of untold millions of people by tempting them to bet money they can't afford to lose. But it's also the greed of those hordes of people who come to Las Vegas anyway, vainly snatching at the money dangled before their eyes. Casino owners try to dress up Las Vegas with elaborate shows, swimming pools, and high-class shops and restaurants. But that doesn't pay for these palaces I see around me. The money comes from gambling, pure and simple. It is the consistent losses, hour by hour, day by day, that eventually add up to these temples of greed.

The next morning I wake up to the sound of the wind rattling the sliding glass doors. I look out and see low, angry clouds. After my morning routine of a shower, some yoga stretches, brain-boosting supplements, and a few hands of computer blackjack, I head to the Aria, which is a quick hike along an elevated walkway. I push open the door and find that rain—yes, rain in Las Vegas—is pelting down. I run for cover and find the Aria is pleasantly deserted. I settle in to a nice two-deck game and go down almost $800. I'm getting that sickening feeling in my stomach until I get a crazy round of a split, a resplit, then two doubles. I win them all and it brings me almost all the way back to even. Finally, I walk away with a $150 loss. This is new to me, the ability to hang in there, and not panic, and then cut a loss down to almost nothing.

I decide to try my own hand at working the system and drop in to check with a casino host in a nearby office.

"I just dropped a couple of hundred at the blackjack tables," I tell the casino host, a well-dressed young guy. "I was hoping you could comp me and a friend for breakfast at the coffee shop."

The host looks me over. It's a quick, brutal glance at my worth—not as a human being—but only in terms of how much money I might be willing to lose. He then rattles the keys of his computer, looking at my action, and finally turns back to me.

"Looks like you've been bangin' it pretty good," he says. "I can comp you for $50 for two. Is that fair?"

"That works, thanks," I say. I know Bill will be happy with the free meal.

I meet up with Bill and we're walking along the crowded hallways, almost to the coffee shop, when we run into another problem. The trouble starts when I begin needling Bill again about how I'm comped in a suite while he had to pay for a room at the Nugget. This is my sense of humor and, frankly, sometimes it rubs people the wrong way. Apparently, this was one of those times.

"Someday, maybe you'll get the big comps," I say.

"Yeah, well, just remember who's winning all the money," he answers, "because it certainly isn't you."

It's such a slap in the face that I almost stop walking. And besides that, it sounded like I was hearing Bill's inner thoughts, his true appraisal of my abilities. I try taking a few deep breaths and just exhaling the negativity. But it doesn't work.

"Wow, Bill—that's really harsh," I say.

"Look on the bright side," he continues. "If the Eye in the Sky was watching you when you stood on 12 against a 10 they'll never think you're counting cards. They took one look at a play like that and they shut down the screens."

"You know what, Bill? I'm doing my best. And you agreed to these terms."

Now he's realizing he might have overdone it.

"I know you are," he says. "And you're doing fine. I'm just kidding around."

But I can't let it go. And we continue the argument over breakfast.

At one point I remember him saying, "You're a smart guy. You'll figure this out."

And I snap back at him. "No, I'm not smart. I might be intelligent but I've never been smart."

That, in a nutshell, is the problem. I always wanted to be one of those guys who did well on quiz shows, who could think of the right answer under pressure. But then I remember something that raises my spirits. When I was in Argentina, studying Spanish, I used to embarrass my son Drew with all the mistakes I made when I talked with the locals. But later in the trip, I met people who knew the language but wouldn't even try to communicate because they were too scared. So I had to give myself credit for pushing forward with my less-than-perfect language skills. My strategy was just to smile and keep talking.

Finally, I just told Drew to relax. "I speak gorilla Spanish," I told him. "And I'm okay with that."

Now, I was playing gorilla blackjack. Still, I know that Bill values our friendship and wants nothing more than to see me succeed. So after breakfast, I take another deep breath and try to let it all go.

I leave Bill at the Wynn and walk across the street to the Treasure Island, where I find a nice $25 minimum table in the high-limit area and score a quick $300 win. When I rejoin Bill he's won $1,400. We're feeling pretty excited about our progress so we sit down and have a cup of coffee. It's about an hour before we need to head to the airport to pick up Father Andy—time to play one more session. An hour later, when we reconnect, I've lost $600 and Bill tells me he lost $2,100. All of a sudden, we're back to even for the day.

We pick up Father Andy at the airport (he flew in a day later because he had to perform a funeral service). We head to the Peppermill and, while we're waiting for a table, I talk one-on-one with the priest. Nearby, Bill pores over the index cards on which he records the results of each session. One particularly important detail he notes is the time of day we play at each casino. There are three shifts each day and it's best to play only once per shift. Still, if we each play at each casino on each shift, that's a lot of opportunities—another good thing about team play.

"I have a friend who sings at funerals," I say to Andy to make conversation. "He said it gave him an insight into death."

"Really?" Andy says, perking up.

"He says that death is a thin veil, that he could sense the spirit of the person who died still hovering in the room."

Andy thinks about this carefully.

"I don't know that I would say that," he replies. "But then again, I'm pretty busy just running the service. It's pretty stressful doing funerals because you can't screw up. If you goof during a wedding everyone just laughs. But every word in a funeral is important. It's like a summary of a person's life for the people who are left living."

He's quiet for a moment and then adds, "There is one thing about doing a funeral service, and I don't want this to seem somehow opportunistic. But at a funeral people are open—emotionally speaking. In some cases they are in a state of extreme anguish and the Church might offer them comfort. I never get that when I do weddings. There, I'm just a fixture."

"So you can give them answers," I say.

He hesitates. "Sometimes there are no answers. For example, I did a service for a young girl. She got drunk and choked to death on her own vomit. What can you say? But the Church is there and I believe it helps people."

It cynically occurs to me that while Andy worships at the Catholic Church, I worship at the Church of Blackjack. During hard times—times of extreme deviation—my faith is tested. But in the long run, winning vindicates the math and righteousness triumphs.

Bill leans over, still fingering the index cards. "After this I figure I'll head back to the Wynn. You can try the high-limit area of Treasure Island—you've done well there. It's the second shift and they may open some more two-deck games."

At Treasure Island I'm relieved to see that I don't recognize the dealer or the pit boss. I decide to try a strategy I discussed with Bill: I'll play one hand of $25 until the count climbs, then I'll spread to two hands of $50 each.

Soon, I'm lost in a long, drawn-out battle of ups and downs. A little later, it turns into a long, slow downhill slide. I lose $500 and I buy in for another $300 and keep playing. Maybe forty-five minutes later I decide it's just not happening and pull back my few remaining chips.

"I took a pretty big hit," I say to the pit boss, a middle-aged man with a distant air. "Do you think I could get a comp for dinner?"

"Where do you want to eat?" he asks, noncommittally.

We talk about the options and he wanders away and begins rattling the keys on his computer. I'm used to this tactic, which is, basically, stalling. I look at my few remaining chips, feel deflated, and wonder how Bill is doing over at the Wynn.

Then, from my right, I hear a voice that sounds like sandpaper.

"You can't play blackjack here anymore."

A stocky, gray-haired man with a face like a mobster leans across the table toward me. He must be the casino manager, called by surveillance after they saw me playing. The dealer has backed away from the table and the pit boss—that coward—is still pathetically rattling the computer keys.

I've heard the casino manager quite clearly, but it's so sudden and unexpected that I say, "Excuse me?"

"You can't play blackjack here anymore," he repeats with a cold stare. Then he snarls: "And we're not giving you any comps either."

I want to push back against this asshole, to innocently ask why, after losing $800, I'm getting this treatment. But from everything I've been told and read in books, it's best to just leave. So I take my chips and march toward the cage. As I walk, a disturbing image jumps into my mind: it's a surveillance screen looking down on me as some faceless security officer watches my action. It's a quick reminder that they are always watching.

All this makes me think of a story that Bill told me once about his early playing days, when the casinos were still controlled by organized crime. He said he had to be careful or he might be back-roomed and beaten for counting cards. But, he said, if you didn't win too much, and treated the dealers and pit bosses with respect, in many ways, the playing conditions were better.

"It was a people business then," Bill says. "Now the place is run by bean counters and they have this nonsense about getting player's cards and accruing points for free rooms and meals."

In the early 1990s, Bill became aware that the casinos were going through a transition. He had developed a relationship with a pit boss named Sal who often gave him generous comps. One day Bill was playing—and winning—when Sal pulled him aside, looking annoyed.

"Bill, you're going to have to cool it for a while."

"What's up?"

"You're winning too much and they're starting to watch you upstairs, okay? So just cool it for a while. Play somewhere else."

"No problem, Sal."

Bill started to walk away when Sal called him back, looking a little apologetic.

"Bill, are you here with your wife?"

"Yeah."

"Listen, I feel kind of bad about this so I want you to take your wife to a nice dinner – on me okay?"

"That's great. Thanks."

"Just give it a couple of weeks and you can play here again. But they were getting nervous so I had to say something to you."

"I understand, Sal. Thanks."

Bill and Pat had a feast at the casino's steakhouse and he avoided that casino for the rest of the trip. The next time Bill was in Las Vegas he went back to the same casino. But Sal wasn't there. He asked one of the dealers what happened to Sal but the dealer said he'd never heard of anyone by that name. After Bill finished playing, and on his way to the cashier, another dealer approached him.

"I couldn't help by overhear you—you were asking Sal, weren't you?" the dealer asked.

"That's right. What happened to him?"

"They let him go," the dealer said. "The new owners, they're making a bunch of changes and they let Sal and a bunch of the old timers go."

"That's a shame," Bill said. "He was a good guy."

"Yeah," the dealer said. "He was a really good guy. But thing are changing around here and I guess there's no more room for guys like Sal."

Bill looked at the dealer, reading into his words.

"Thanks for letting me know."

As I walk out of the Treasure Island, and into the heat of a Las Vegas summer, I try to feel excited about accomplishing the goal of being backed off. It means the casino thinks I'm good enough to be a threat. But then it hits me that just when I'm getting good enough to count cards and win money, the game changes. It's no longer a question of can I win money. It's now about trying to win money while making it look like dumb luck.

Chapter 23

Sweet Revenge

"Blackjack is unique among all casino games in that it is a game in which skill should make a difference, even swing the odds in the player's favor. Because of the possibilities of using information and exercising rational choice, this game has an appeal to many who wouldn't ordinarily be interested in gambling."

—Peter A. Griffin, *The Theory of Blackjack*

The next morning I'm still smarting from yesterday's losses so I head to Mandalay Bay in search of an open table. I like sitting on the backside of the pit because there is less foot traffic behind me and fewer players trying to jump into the game. I find an open table but, as I approach, I see there's a problem: it's the Afghan dealer, the exotic beauty who—a year ago—not only took $500 from me, but she also complained to the pit boss that I was confused and trying to change my bets in mid-deal.

I take another lap around the pit hoping to find another open table. But when I return the Afghan woman is still there, waiting for the next player. A lot has happened in the past year and I decide it's time for some redemption.

I take a seat.

She glances at me but doesn't remember me. But I remember her quite well. And I remember the shame I felt when my gaffes were announced to the pit boss: "He's confused and trying to raise his bets when I'm already dealing."

But now I'm back, sitting alone, my mind sharpened by a year of playing experience. Looking at the woman's striking, imposing face, I'm daunted by the memory of that humiliating encounter. And then, as if a voice in my head is giving me the encouragement that Bill usually supplies, I hear an inner voice: "This is about overcoming fear." It strikes me that this whole adventure has been to learn to overcome my fear and my superstition. This past year has presented many moments like this, when I had to face my fear and move forward anyway.

I buy in with $500 and the shoe begins. I'm up and down for a few hands. Suddenly, a shadow falls across the table. A huge guy appears behind me along with a woman, presumably his wife. He throws a couple of green chips on the table but doesn't take a seat.

"Can you wait to the end of the shoe?" I ask, keeping the count on my fingers below the table.

"I don't speak English," he growls. However, he says this in perfect English, so it's probably just his clever way of blowing off people like me.

Now we're both playing and the cards still aren't going anywhere. I'm hoping the guy leaves after the shuffle but, no, he is still standing there, draped over the chair, throwing green chips across the table. The dealer is ready to start and waits for me to put out a bet.

"You mind if I sit out a few hands?" I ask the dealer as she prepares to start the new shoe.

"Not at all," she says, perhaps sensing my annoyance with this hulking stranger.

I sit back, basically hoping this guy crashes and burns. But then it occurs to me: this is a perfect time to try "Wonging"—keeping the count without betting. Sure enough, the guy is getting all low cards and the count shoots up into positive territory. A few hands later he snatches up his small win and leaves the table without even a grunt of thanks. Meanwhile, I jump back in with twin bets of $100 and win both hands.

Seconds later, two more guys sit down with me.

"Do you mind waiting for the reshuffle?" I ask.

They turn out to be more accommodating than the non-English-speaking stranger. "No problem," they say, and sit back to watch.

The count is still so high I put a hundred on each hand. And suddenly I start winning everything. The new guys sitting at my table are cheering me on and congratulating me every time I have a successful hit. It's unbelievable. If I have a 16 I hit and get a 5 for a 21. If I double on 9 I get an ace for a 20. If she is showing an ace I take insurance and win.

"That was the shoe of a lifetime!" one guy says as I finish.

Yes it was, I think. *But not for the reasons you think.*

Meanwhile, the pit boss, who looks like an enforcer off the streets of Brooklyn, comes over and frowns at the chips, calculating my win, which is $735. One of my new friends reads his expression and says, "Uh-oh. They don't like it when you win."

Later that day I leave Father Andy and Bill at the Encore. I play and win $320 at the Wynn from a dealer who keeps chirping, "Easy money!" every time I win a hand. I then walk over to the Mirage, where I am moving for the night since the Cosmo comp is only good for two nights. I find an open table there and win another $550 in two quick shoes.

By now I am becoming comfortable playing at the $50 level, with two hands. The $50 tables keep a lot of other players away, and it also means that I can win a significant amount in just one shoe rather than go up and down a little for hours. Because of the math, it is much more likely that the wins shoot up, rather than down, which is what is happening to me.

With a nice wad of bills in my pocket, I head to the registration desk at the Mirage to claim my free room. Behind the check-in counter is a huge aquarium and right behind the head of this nice young check-in lady is a gigantic moray eel that is swirling around in a psychedelic fashion. The clerk tells me that unless I want to upgrade to a suite, I can't check in until later. I'm a little dizzy from the moray eel behind her head, but I tell her I'll wait and check in later. After a few more minutes of rattling the computer keys she says, "You know what? I just went ahead and upgraded you for free." I respond by giving her a $10 bill. I'm a big tipper when I'm winning.

The check-in experience makes me feel like a high roller, like Vegas is opening its arms to me, that the secret life that Bill promised me is finally arriving. I go up to my suite on the twenty-fourth floor and pour the money out of my pockets. It's just paper, I tell myself, and yet the sight of all those bills does something to me. I stretch out on the bed and fall into a deep, lucid dreaming state.

After my power nap, I return to the Encore. I call Bill and he tells me he's playing at a table in the corner. He asks me to find Father Andy, who's playing video poker nearby, and meet him at the table. I find Andy and we walk toward the table wondering if we should maintain our distance. But Bill enthusiastically waves us over. A soft-spoken middle-aged woman is dealing to Bill as the pit boss, a younger Asian woman, looks on. He has a small stack of black chips in front of him and apparently has established a great rapport with both women. The dealer, in her quiet way, is rooting for Bill and calls him by name.

"Okay, Bill," she says. "This shoe is going to turn things around."

"I hope so," Bill laughs. "I'm down about two grand."

As the new cards come out, I stand to the side and watch with Andy. Bill puts $300 on each of two hands. He gets a double down and now has $900 on the table. The dealer lays out one card after another then busts with a total of 22. I look over at Andy, who flaps the front of his shirt, pretending he is fanning away the sweat.

"I could never do what Bill does," Andy says. "I'd have a coronary. I'm terrified just watching."

"I know what you mean," I say. "But I have seen him come back so many times I'm starting to relax and enjoy the show."

Meanwhile, Bill's had a good shoe and he's back up.

"I didn't do all this work just to win five hundred bucks," Bill says. "Come on, Maurine, let's have another good shoe."

"I'll do my best, Bill," the dealer says.

Watching the cards, I think back to my ruminations two nights ago about how greed built the casinos of Las Vegas. I share my thought with Father Andy as we watch the game continue. He ponders my words carefully.

"To me it's all about risk," Andy says.

"What do you mean?"

"It's like watching a ball game and hearing the crack of the bat and seeing the ball take off. Or it's about a three-pointer while the basketball is still in the air. In that moment, anything could happen, and you're in a state of complete involvement."

"Right," I say, connecting with his thoughts and feeling pinpricks of excitement. "Only here in Las Vegas, it's about the roll of the dice. Or it's like that moment when you've doubled your bets and get a 20 and the dealer is showing a 10. What's the dealer's hole card? Will the dealer beat your 20 or bust?"

There's a buzz of excitement from the table and we look to see that Bill is putting down a $5 bet on one hand for the dealer.

"Come on, Maurine," Bill says. "Let's both win. Hang on!" He puts out another bet and turns to the pit boss. "I want to get you in this game too."

"Thanks! And we've got a good chance," the pit boss says. "There're five more aces left."

The pit boss is uncharacteristically involved—and even helpful. But then again, here at the Wynn, they don't sweat your action. To this casino, Bill is playing for chicken feed.

"You're counting aces?" Bill is surprised. "You should be on this side of the table."

"It's safer over here," she says, laughing.

Instead of watching the cards, I find myself watching the faces of the two women, the dealer and the pit boss. Even with this modest wager on the table, they are transformed. The pit boss, in particular, leans in expectantly. *Maybe Andy is right*, I think. *In this moment of suspense—of risk—with the future unknown, there is no past and no future. Only that place of serenity we are all trying to reach—the now.*

Bill has a 17 and a 15 and stands against the dealer's 6. But she flips her hole card to reveal a 5, making her total 11.

"Uh-oh" the pit boss says, knowing full well that a 10 is likely for a 21.

"Small card," Bill says softly.

The dealer lays out a 4 for a 15.

"Out," Bill says determinedly.

But the dealer then lays out an ace for a 16. The pit boss makes a quiet whimpering sound.

"Out!" Bill says again.

"Picture," the pit boss moans, begging for a face card.

If this was a movie, we would see a close-up shot of the dealer's hand, turning the next card in slow motion. The card would be blurred, but we could see it's not the face card that could bust her. Instead, it has spots and numbers. But how many? A 5, 4, or 3 would all be death.

The cards lands and the camera zooms in. It's a 6 for 22 and the dealer busts. Everyone wins! The pit boss jumps back and her face lights up in a smile. Bill high-fives the dealer.

I turn to Andy, who is flapping his shirt again.

"I need a shower," he says.

When the dealer colors up Bill's chips he has a nice $1,400 win.

That night we take a break from cards and go to see Shania Twain at Caesar's Coliseum. Before the show starts Bill runs through his index cards and tells me my cut of the winnings so far is $1,600.

The Shania Twain show is cheesy but fun. She arrives in a blast of music, lowered from the ceiling on a thundering chrome motor-cycle. Afterward, we head out into the casino and look for an open table for a last session. But it is an utter madhouse, busier than an airport just before Thanksgiving. We go back to the Wynn. There, Bill sees an open $100 table.

"You want in on this as team play?" Bill asks. "Or do you want to just stick with the $1,600 win?"

"With you playing, I'd be a fool to say no," I answer.

Two shoes later, he cashes out with about $1,400.

"I could have won more," he says. "But I've got to be careful. I've won about thirty grand here over the past two years. I don't want to push my luck."

After a trip to the cage he hands me my share—four $100 bills. Now my win is a cool $2,000.

We have a farewell glass of Pinot Noir—free, of course—as we sit among the slot machines. Bill and Andy are catching an early flight the next morning and they're going to the airport by cab.

"You going to play anymore tomorrow?" Bill asks. "You've got a pretty good bankroll now."

"I was thinking about that," I answer. "I could play at the Mirage and Bellagio. Then hit the Aria and play my way out of town."

"Look at you," Bill says, laughing. "You've got it all figured out."

I sleep deeply that night—until about 4 a.m. Then, the relief and satisfaction of the day's wins evaporate. I wake up knowing there are open tables downstairs and I'll soon have to play and face the consequences. I go back to sleep but now I'm fitful, the apprehension and excitement beginning to gnaw my guts like evil squirrels hyped up on Red Bull. And then there is a special doubt that creeps in on the final morning of a trip. I have only a few more hours before I head home. I can play another session or two and that might sweeten my winnings. But there is the very real chance that I could backslide or dig a hole and leave Las Vegas depressed.

Finally, I decide, what the hell, I've got an open day and lots of money. Besides, fortune favors the bold. After all, unless I plan to quit playing forever, then blackjack—like life—is really just one long session.

The tables downstairs at the Mirage are open and the dealers and pit boss are standing around, idle. This pit boss is the opposite of what the name conjures up: she's a pleasant, chunky, middle-aged woman in a pants suit who looks like a hall monitor in middle school.

I buy in with $500 and play two hands of $50 against the dealer. I begin winning right away. I win so much I think this will be a record-breaking shoe for me. Toward the last hand, I decide to imitate Bill. I tell the dealer and pit boss I'm putting out a bet for each of them—$5 on each of the two hands. Only this time, I catch a double on each hand. I double for them both and now they have $10 in play. After a flurry of small cards, the dealer busts and we all win. Suddenly, we're like a happy team that just won a basketball game with a buzzer-beater.

When I tip the dealer he thanks me for including something for the pit boss. He lowers his voice and leans across the table: "Jenny is trying to scrape enough together to buy health insurance."

I glance over at Jenny and she morphs from a threatening pit boss into a human being, someone struggling to make ends meet, just like anyone else. I'm glad I included her and even more relieved the bet got her a nice tip.

When I cash out I find I have won another $490—in just one shoe. So my total for two and a half days of blackjack is almost $2,500. Not only that, but I'm up about $4,000 for the year—almost halfway to my 2013 goal of $10,000—and we're only a third of the way through the year.

When I have a successful trip, such as this one, it glows in my mind for several days. When I talk with Bill by phone a few days later, something pops into my mind.

"How would you describe our winnings?" I ask him.

"We won about six grand," he says. "I'd call that pretty average."

"You know, in the past, I've experienced a lot of negative variance," I say. "But I guess there can also be positive variance too."

"Without a doubt," he agrees. "I've had trips where I flew back with so much money I didn't know where to put it."

Leaving Las Vegas

"Man, I wonder what that would be like."

"Keep playing," he answers. "And you'll find out."

It's a week after New Year's and I drive to Las Vegas to meet my father, who is flying in from his home in snowbound Massachusetts. I get into town early, play one warm-up session at the El Cortez, and win a quick and effortless $275. I pick up my dad and we settle into a comped suite at the Cosmopolitan.

The next morning I take to the tables.

From the Cosmo, it's an easy walk to the Aria to the south, and the Bellagio to the north. As I bounce back and forth between casinos I check in with Dad, who is sitting on the suite's couch, happily reading and writing emails on his iPad. Whenever I return to the room he greets me with a hearty, "How did you do?" When I answer, he shakes his head in amazement and smiles proudly.

I'm not in full-out attack mode, like my trips with Bill. It's just a relaxed series of short sessions. I'm playing the $25 six-deck games, usually keeping my bets low until there is only one deck left to play. Then, if the count is high, I spread to two hands and raise my bets. By the end of the afternoon I've won about $900.

Late in the afternoon, my dad gets restless and wants to get in on the fun. So, after a comped meal, we head over to the Bellagio. My dad is eighty-seven years old now and he walks slower and is more stooped than before his fall down the stairs. But he walks without a cane and still has a twinkle in his eye as he watches his son "fleece the casinos." Sometimes, though, he grows sad and complains about how the years have taken their toll. So I finally tell him, "Dad, it's nothing short of a miracle that you're walking at all. Not one man in a hundred could do what you've done after a fall like that."

He straightens up and for a few minutes walks with a spring in his step.

Pushing through the revolving door into the Bellagio, it's busy, even though it's a Monday night. Word has it there's a convention of builders in town. Of course, there's always a convention of some kind in town. Middle-aged guys pack the tables. They are refugees from the snows of the Northeast and Midwest, still wearing name tags and looking like they're totally off the chain.

Dad and I find a six-deck game with a $25 minimum, which has room for us both to sit at the table. When I travel with Dad, people smile knowingly at me and go out of their way to accommodate us. Dad orders a margarita and I ask for a Coors Light, since it has the lowest alcohol content of any beer and won't dull the accuracy of my card counting. I'm watching the count climb as Freddy, a handsome, charismatic dealer from El Salvador, flips out a stream of low cards. I catch a 9 and a 2 for 11 and Freddy shows a 10. I double down and have $50 riding on the bet.

"I'm going to hit that one hard," Freddy tells me. He gives me a 10 for 21 and flips over his hole card to show he's got 20.

"Wow!" my dad exclaims. "You needed every bit of that."

"Didn't I tell you I'd hit it hard?" Freddy says, and fist bumps my dad.

"Oh boy! You sure did!" my dad laughs.

At the end of the shoe I'm up $250.

"Dad, let's get going," I say. It's that old fear that if I stay too long, it will all go backward. And I want to walk away a winner in my dad's eyes.

"Why're you leaving?" Dad asks. "You're way ahead. And Freddy's a great dealer."

"Thanks so much, Tom," Freddy replies with great dignity. They've known each other for twenty minutes, but now they're like soul mates.

"Okay. One more shoe," I tell him. But he's not listening. A gorgeous cocktail waitress has stopped at our table. She flashes a brilliant smile for my dad and bends toward him, giving him a nice shot of some world-class cleavage.

"Gentlemen?" she murmurs, still smiling at my dad.

My dad finally recovers his voice. "I'm going to be naughty and have just one more margarita."

"I like naughty," she answers, and squeezes his arm. She walks away and my dad's eyes follow her. I can't help but think she is putting a little extra swing in her hips for his benefit.

The count starts to rise in about the middle of the shoe. I spread to two hands and double my bets.

"He's making a big play here," Freddy says to my dad. He deals me an ace on one hand and a jack on the other.

"Nice start," my dad says as I think again how wonderful it is that, when the count climbs, the high cards magically appear. At least, that's the way it's supposed to work. And when it actually happens, it's like I'm seeing into the future.

But I'm not ready for what happens next. Freddy lays a king on my ace and an ace on my jack for two blackjacks. Freddy cheers. My dad almost falls off his chair. And then, as the excitement dies down, I hear another voice. Only this voice is in my head. It's Bill's quiet, patient voice, from months ago as we practiced card counting in his basement.

"When the count is high, you might catch two blackjacks—boom, boom!" I remember him saying. "When that happens you want to have your big money out there."

Bill also looked into the future. It was my future, and he helped me create it.

We leave Las Vegas the next morning and I've got $1,300 of *their* money in my pocket. We drive the long route back through Death Valley and I have a lot of time to reflect on my year in the pits—that is, the blackjack pits. I find myself pondering how I would answer anyone who asked me if card counting is worth learning. And what I learned about myself while learning to beat the casinos.

First, a few stats. I've taken five trips to Las Vegas over the course of the year. I've also played in Tunica, and Biloxi, Mississippi, as well as St. Louis and various Indian casinos across California. All told, I've played about sixty separate sessions, winning just over half of them. However, my winnings have totaled $6,100. By itself, that's not very impressive. However, it proves that card counting works. It means you have a positive expectation, something not available in any other casino game. If I had merely played basic strategy for the sixty sessions, I would have been negative. Now, I'm solidly positive.

So, has it been worth it? On the one hand, I had to buy plane tickets to the two Mississippi destinations. But I rarely paid for hotels and I got a lot of comped meals. I did spend a lot of time away from my family, alone in hotels and on the road. It was stressful, exciting, and illuminating. And it showed me a lot about myself, my attitude toward money, and the way my brain works.

Learning to count cards has been more difficult than I ever imagined. Bill taught himself, using books. But I could have never gotten to this level of ability without Bill's patient instruction and his hands-on support. After many brutal losses and negative trips I might have just hung it up altogether. But he kept me coming back and the payoff is a trip like this one, which gave me a nice, steady series of wins.

For those who are determined to play blackjack at a higher level, or learn to count cards, I have two suggestions.

For the occasional traveler to Las Vegas, you can greatly improve your performance at blackjack by mastering every single play of basic strategy. Practice until you can automatically recall every single split, double down, and soft double under pressure. Then, learn to play within your bankroll and resist the temptation to play hunches, chase your bets, or suddenly "go all-in." Even if you don't want to actually count cards, you can still improve your chances by looking for a flood of low cards before you raise your bets. This means the high cards are probably coming on the next hand.

If you decide to learn to count cards, I suggest taking a year to master the skill. Begin with a simple count such as the Knock Out. You can later move up to the Hi-Lo and then the Hi-Opt 1 that uses an ace side count. Practice by counting down a deck of cards over and over again until you can do it in thirty seconds with no mistakes. Install a blackjack app on your phone and play while you're standing in line at the store. Work hard to make basic strategy absolutely automatic so you can devote the higher levels of your mind to the count, making betting decisions and interacting naturally with the dealer and pit boss.

Once you feel you're ready for the casino, proceed slowly and don't get either discouraged by early losses or overconfident from quick wins—they are both deceiving. Never forget how powerful and ruthless the casino system is. Even though the dealer is friendly and sympathetic, she is the face of a black-hearted corporation, dedicated to grinding you down and taking every last dollar from your wallet.

And never, ever forget that the Eye in the Sky is watching you.

As for me and my own blackjack future, it's all up in the air. I'm sure that Bill and I will take more trips with many more peaks and valleys. We've talked about finding investors and playing out of a bigger bankroll. Meanwhile, I'm amazed—and very proud—that I've even gotten to this level. I recall listening to Bill describe his trips with other counters: meeting at the Peppermill for breakfast, then splitting up and hitting the blackjack tables, texting each other after their wins. Now, I'm that guy. I can count cards. I can win money more often than not.

Learning to count cards was a self-assigned test for me, and a chance for redemption. What I discovered is that I can learn a difficult, complex task. However, I might learn more slowly than other people, using different methods, and require more practice. I wish I had learned back in high school instead of simply letting the system brand me as a poor student. We are all different, with different brain architecture, but the educational system treats us the same.

This year also taught me that I can—at this age—learn a difficult skill and perform under pressure. The challenge, the practice, and the actual contest has left my brain feeling more flexible even as my peers complain of forgetfulness and slowed reactions. It takes constant mental exercise, plus a healthy diet and plenty of exercise. But you definitely can—as the magazine title suggested—"Buff Your Brain."

When I think of how far I've come, I wish that Miss Reid, my math teacher from years ago, could see her former student, who once stood frozen at the blackboard staring at a difficult problem as mocking laughter rang through the class. I won't say that I am smart, but I sure feel that way when I walk away from the blackjack table with a handful of chips.

As I look back over these pages I see that all this was really a journey of self-discovery. The revelation is that I'm not the person I thought I was. If you took such a journey, I'm sure there would be many surprises for you, too. I invite you to give yourself a similar challenge. It certainly doesn't have to be in a casino, but it should be something that urges you to confront your fears because, as I've learned, the best response to fear is to go straight at it. And when you do, you will find, as I did, that there is something that goes along with you, and gives you the strength to win.

The End